A Wargamer's Guide to The Desert War 1940–1943

About the Author

Daniel Mersey has written several sets of miniatures rules and has been a regular contributor to hobby magazines since the mid 1990s. Although best known for his writing on the medieval and colonial periods, the Desert War has long held a fascination for him. Like many gamers, he can trace this interest back to the endless boyhood fun gifted by unpainted Airfix Eighth Army and Afrika Korps toy soldiers and a boundless fascination with Desert War tanks.

A Wargamer's Guide to The Desert War 1940–1943

By Daniel Mersey

Pen & Sword
MILITARY

First published in Great Britain in 2017 by
Pen & Sword Military
an imprint of
Pen & Sword Books Ltd
47 Church Street
Barnsley
South Yorkshire
S70 2AS

ISBN 978 1 47385 108 5

Typeset in Ehrhardt by
Mac Style Ltd, Bridlington, East Yorkshire
Printed and bound in Malta by Gutenberg Press Ltd.

Pen & Sword Books Ltd incorporates the imprints of Pen & Sword
Archaeology, Atlas, Aviation, Battleground, Discovery, Family
History, History, Maritime, Military, Naval, Politics, Railways, Select,
Transport, True Crime, and Fiction, Frontline Books, Leo Cooper,
Praetorian Press, Seaforth Publishing and Wharncliffe.

For a complete list of Pen & Sword titles please contact
PEN & SWORD BOOKS LIMITED
47 Church Street, Barnsley, South Yorkshire, S70 2AS, England
E-mail: enquiries@pen-and-sword.co.uk
Website: www.pen-and-sword.co.uk

Contents

Acknowledgements

Thanks to historical researcher Simon Bell for his assistance, input, and ability to debus motorized infantry in front of my machine guns. I'm also extremely grateful to all those kind souls who offered photos for this book, whether I was able to use them or not. Photo credits are listed in the captions for each image.

Introduction

From the early, amateurish exploits of the British and Italians in 1940, through Rommel's initial success, to the Axis retreat from North Africa in 1943, the Second World War's desert campaign provides wargamers with visually distinctive, exciting tactical challenges, and a whole host of armour and equipment to deploy on the battlefield.

Many gamers describe the Desert War as the Second World War in its purest strategic and tactical form, unrestricted by civilian population and fought across a seemingly limitless expanse of land – so long as your supply line remained intact.

Paddy Griffith described the war in North Africa as a tough testing ground for military theorists:

> It was pure mechanized warfare, and as such it was the long-awaited test for many of the futuristic theories and speculations that had been put forward during the 1920s and 1930s. At first sight the open desert terrain seemed to be 'good tank country' or even a 'tactician's dream' ... Alas for all this optimistic idealism, it soon became apparent that before 1940 very few European soldiers had had the slightest idea of what this terrain was really like – especially not from the point of view of large-scale mechanized warfare.
>
> (Paddy Griffith, *World War II Desert Tactics*, 2008, pp. 3–4)

The North African campaign – to give the 'Desert War' it's proper title – combined three areas of operation:

- Western Desert Campaign (Libya and Egypt, June 1940 to February 1943).

- Operation Torch (Morocco and Algeria, November 1942).
- Tunisian Campaign (Tunisia, November 1942 to May 1943).

Covering nearly three years of the entire six year conflict, the war in the desert inevitably changed in scope and method over time, beginning as a fairly ad hoc encounter between British and Italian forces – seemingly blundering around the desert looking for one another – but progressing over time to become a series of set-piece operations between combined arms forces with increasingly sophisticated equipment and tactics.

Aside from the epic confrontation between the Germans and Soviet Union on the Eastern Front, the Desert War offers the greatest variety of equipment and tactical challenges in the Second World War. Above all else, it offers the wargamer plenty of opportunities to field a whole swathe of different tanks, from the slightly obscure and wholly ineffective Italian L6/40 and British Mk VI light tanks through to the famous American Sherman and German Tiger.

This book is an introduction to wargaming the campaign, so it's written with the gamer in mind, not the military historian. It's about playing games, so I try not to dwell upon the kind of information easily available in the many good accounts of the desert war that you'll find on the shelves of any worthwhile bookstore (and in the pages of the stacks of wargame rules you will almost certainly end up amassing). This is especially true of the real-life formations and regiments who fought in the desert and blow-by-blow accounts of the major battles (each could be a wargaming book in its own right) … instead I concentrate on presenting the information you need to help you to collect and field your armies, and then to play through an enjoyable game on your tabletop. I encompass the game-relevant historical details you'll need to get started in the period as a hobby, or to reignite interest in a collection of models that you already own. But a book of this length cannot cover everything: the further reading list at the end of the book, and the list of rules I suggest trying out, supply further ammunition for your campaign in north Africa.

Happy gaming!

A note of clarification: Where I refer to 'British' forces, please consider this a shorthand description of both British and Commonwealth units, who mostly shared the same equipment, organization, and tactics. Within this catch-all word are included Indian, Rhodesian, South African, Australian, New Zealand, and Canadian troops, plus units from other Commonwealth countries.

Similarly, I use 'Afrika Korps' to describe German forces for the sake of consistency; the official title of German forces in North Africa changed several times as the original Afrika Korps grew in size and incorporated Italian units: Panzer Group Africa (Panzergruppe Afrika, Gruppo Corazzato Africa), August 1941–January 1942; Panzer Army Africa (Panzerarmee Afrika, Armata Corazzata Africa), January–October 1942; German-Italian Panzer Army (Deutsch-Italienische Panzerarmee, Armata Corazzata Italo-Tedesca), October 1942–February 1943; Army Group Africa (Heeresgruppe Afrika, Gruppo d'Armate Africa), February–May 1943.

Chapter One

The Desert War

The North African campaign of 1940 to 1943 was fought between armies that seem to have been permanently teetering on the edge of disaster. Dominated by considerations of supply and attrition, it was contested using often obsolescent equipment and in the most extreme conditions of heat and aridity possible. With huge possibilities for manoeuvre in what was literally a sandbox, it saw extraordinary achievements by often ad hoc forces exploiting tactical situations which changed with bewildering speed.

When Mussolini declared war on Britain and France on 10 June 1940, it is probably fair to say that he caught his forces in North Africa at least as much by surprise as he did his enemies. In Libya, which had been an Italian possession since just before the First World War, the local commander was Marshal of the Air Force, Italo Balbo, who was also Governor General of Libya. Under his overall command were the 5th Army, based in the western half of Libya (Tripolitania), and the 10th Army, based in the eastern half of the country (Cyrenaica) and directly facing the British forces in Egypt. The 5th Army, with eight infantry divisions, was commanded by General Italo Gariboldi; the six-division 10th Army was led by General Mario Berti.

Neither force was in peak condition. Pre-war reforms designed to help the Italian army respond more quickly to fast-changing mobile warfare had actually had the reverse effect, causing administrative bottlenecks which severely hampered the military's logistical capability. In a war in which logistical considerations would prove crucial, this was a serious handicap. Nonetheless, the manpower the Italians could put into the field was impressive: there were perhaps 215,000 Italian troops in Libya as hostilities commenced.

Facing the Italians to the east was the much smaller British command. At the outbreak of the campaign, the British and Commonwealth forces in Egypt numbered about 36,000 men, with a further 25–30,000 being trained in Palestine and gradually making their way into the front line. The force was under the overall command of Lieutenant-General Archibald Wavell, GOC-in-Chief of the relatively newly-minted Middle East Command. Other significant senior commanders included Major-General Percy Hobart, commanding the Mobile Division (Egypt), an armoured training formation which subsequently became the 7th Armoured Division, and the formidable Major-General Richard O'Connor, who commanded the 6th Infantry Division, renamed the Western Desert Force (WDF) in June 1940.

The disparity in numerical strengths between the British and Italians concealed the truth of the situation: the British formations had superior equipment and logistics, and a command structure which, if sometimes indecisive, was at least not riven with the infighting which plagued the Italians.

The first hostilities took place in June 1940, immediately after the Italian declaration of war, when British forces including the 11th Hussars (mounted in Rolls-Royce armoured cars) advanced across the Libyan frontier wire and seized the forts at Capuzzo and Maddalena on the 14th. These gains were not held for long, owing to the problems of logistics and manpower involved in maintaining troops there, but this raid was the first significant action of the Desert War. Nonetheless, the overall British position remained broadly defensive.

Italian plans for an initial large-scale offensive in the opposite direction were hampered by a series of mishaps and delays. On 28th June, Marshal Balbo was killed when the aircraft in which he was travelling was shot down by friendly fire over Tobruk. His replacement, Marshal Rodolfo Graziani, was given a deadline of 8th August to begin the offensive against the British for which Balbo had been preparing. However Graziani, perhaps appreciating more keenly than his political masters the actual state of Italian forces in North Africa, sought to delay operations for as long as he could, requesting extra supplies and logistical support. Three deadlines were set for the beginning of the offensive, (15th July, 22nd August and 9

September), and each time it was cancelled as Graziani prevaricated. It was only when he was threatened with demotion that he finally put plans into action, with the drive east beginning on 13th September 1940.

The plan was for infantry divisions of XXIII Corps of 10th Army to advance along the coast, seizing the key Halfaya Pass and advancing on the initial objective of Sidi Barrani. Simultaneously, a mechanized force, the Maletti Group, would advance south and east into the desert to add width to the offensive. With a position established at Sidi Barrani, the 10th Army would consolidate, beat off an anticipated British counterattack, and then press on to take the main British garrison position at Mersa Matruh.

The operation (dubbed Operazione E) did not get off to an auspicious start. The mechanized Maletti Group, consisting of three motorized infantry battalions and substantial armoured forces, got lost in the desert before it had even reached the frontier. Lacking proper maps and navigational equipment, it had to be guided back on track by aircraft. Elsewhere, things went better. The important objective of the Halfaya Pass (Hellfire Pass to British veterans) was secured despite a short delaying action by units of the Coldstream Guards and the Northumberland Fusiliers. Despite harassment from greatly numerically inferior British forces, the advance rolled on, and by 16 September the 23rd Marzo Blackshirt Division had occupied Sidi Barrani.

That was as far as they got. The Italian forces, having advanced at infantry pace some 60 miles into Egypt, dug in, preparing a series of five fortified camps around Sidi Barrani. There was to be no immediate gathering of forces for a potentially decisive strike against Mersa Matruh, with its potential harvest of 25,000 British prisoners. Instead, Graziani embarked on a much more leisurely build-up of forces, bringing further armoured units across to Libya and massing for another frontal assault planned for December. He did so much to the exasperation of Mussolini, and his relationship with the 10th Army commander, Berti, descended into a feud. Graziani's relative inaction was further promoted by the Italian decision to attack Greece in October; with this distraction, Graziani could continue his languid preparations with less pressure from Mussolini.

The British response to this Italian incursion was rather more forthright. By December 1940, plans had been prepared by the British to push back the Italians from Sidi Barrani and exploit any potential for follow-up operations, Originally intended as a five-day raid, the counter-strike, named Operation Compass, would develop into one of the most spectacular successes of the Western Desert campaign.

The offensive began, following extensive reconnaissance, on 9 December 1940, with an assault on the fortified camps surrounding Sidi Barrani by the 7th Armoured Division, 4th Indian Division and the 16th Infantry Brigade. At Nibeiwa, where the attack first fell, the Italian local commander General Pietro Maletti was killed and the camp seized by the 11th Indian Infantry Brigade with support from 7th Royal Tank Regiment (RTR). By nightfall on the 9th, the camps at Tummar East and West had fallen as well. The following day, the British swept on to Sidi Barrani, where the Italian defensive force were pocketed and surrendered by nightfall, the action involving 16th Infantry Brigade and the 'Selby Force', a mixed motorized detachment based around the 3rd Battalion, the Coldstream Guards. The surrender of Italian forces in Sidi Barrani brought the Allies more than 38,000 prisoners, 70 tanks and close to 300 guns.

Allied success snowballed. The main command of the Italian 10th Army was away to the west in Bardia, and in no position to effectively co-ordinate a defence. The Italians abandoned the settlements of Rabia and Sofafi, and the 7th Armoured Division pushed eastwards along the coast and along the high ground inland.

Bardia fell to the Australian 6th Division on 5 January 1941, following a dawn attack from the west that began on the 3rd. Again, large numbers of prisoners were taken and a vast amount of materiel captured.

With Italian forces now in full westward retreat, Tobruk was the next target, and it fell to Australian troops on 22 January after an attack beginning the previous day. Benghazi followed on 6 February, taken by another ad hoc cross-country flying column, 'Combe Force', named after its commander, Lieutenant-Colonel JFB Combe. This force had been assembled out of wheeled vehicles, because the mountainous going south of the main coast road made it difficult for armour to operate. Having cut off the Italian forces south of Benghazi, and after a fierce and sometimes desperate engagement at Beda Fomm, Combe Force, with support from 4th Armoured Brigade and 7th Support, forced the surrender of 10th Army and took Benghazi. Major-General O'Connor, commander of XIII was keen to press on and deal with the Italians in Tripolitania (western Libya), and Wavell agreed, but circumstances beyond their control were about to take a hand.

By the time Churchill ordered its halt at El Agheila, Operation Compass, originally conceived as a five-day raid, had developed into one of the most successful Allied offensives of the war, lasting three months and delivering a staggering dividend. The Italian 10th Army had lost at least 5,500 men killed, 10,000 wounded and 133,298 taken prisoner; losses of materiel included 420 tanks and 845 guns. British casualties were around 10 per cent of their opponents', although they had also suffered significant losses in vehicles, armour and aircraft, mostly to the hostile operating conditions. Not for the first or last time, attrition and over-extended supply lines had brought a successful campaign to its end. And Operation Compass would prove to be the high-water mark of Allied success for over a year.

The reasons for the subsequent Allied reverses of 1941 are complex but ultimately come down to two main factors: Greece and Rommel. Only a few days after the success at Beda Fomm, orders came through from London to hold the gains in Libya with greatly reduced forces, while transferring the bulk of the troops who had achieved the successes of Compass to Greece, as an expeditionary force to try to hold back the imminent German invasion of the peninsula. This force would include the 6th Australian Division, whose role in the pursuit phase of Compass had been crucial.

If the loss of so many seasoned troops left a huge hole in terms of manpower and logistics, then the tactical situation was also about to turn dramatically against the Allies. On 11 January 1941, as the Italian disaster in Cyrenaica unfolded, Hitler signed off Directive 22, pledging 'German support for battles in the Mediterranean area'. A month later, Hitler installed Erwin Rommel as the commander of the newly formed Afrika Korps, and troops began to arrive in Libya from 10 February. Unternehmen Sonnenblume (Operation Sunflower) was underway, and within a dramatically short period had turned the tables on the Allies.

The Afrika Korps was a triumph of improvisation. Hitler had not initially intended to fight in Africa, and might well never have intervened had it not been for the Italian capitulation. The force – as with several others in the theatre – was a make-do-and-mend collection of units. The 5th Light Division (subsequently 21st Panzer) was raised from elements of other Panzer formations, as was the 15th Panzer Division. Their equipment, while at least as good as the Allies', was basically what was deemed surplus to requirements in Operation Barbarossa, the German invasion of Russia, the build up to which began in May 1941, and which had occupied so much of Hitler's strategic thinking.

Despite the success of Compass, and because of the departure of the Greek force, the Allied position in Libya was desperately weak. Cyrenaica (eastern Libya, broadly speaking) was held by Cyrenaica Command (Cyrcom, under Lieutenant-General Henry Maitland Wilson); this consisted of the 9th Australian Division and the 2nd Armoured Division (less a brigade group which had been sent to Greece). Lieutenant-General Richard O'Connor, one of the leading lights of Compass as commander of XXIII Corps, took over command in Egypt. Wavell, the Commander-in-Chief Middle East, and the GHQ in Egypt both believed that the Germans could not be ready for offensive operations until May, by which time the 2nd Armoured Division tanks would have been refitted and two more divisions and support artillery would be in place, along with the 9th Australian Division. Rommel swiftly disabused them of this idea.

The Afrika Korps offensive began on 24 March 1941 with an attack on Allied positions at El Agheila and on the positions of the 3rd Armoured Brigade near Mersa Brega, forcing a British withdrawal. Two Italian divisions of the 5th Army also advanced from Tripoli. Hampered by overextended lines and poor communications, the Allied commanders compounded their weakened starting position with a confused reaction, and by 6 April, a general withdrawal was ordered. In truth, Rommel had his own problems, with fuel shortages soon becoming critical, but the Allies were not able to take advantage of this weakness, partly through poor intelligence, but also through their own worsening logistical position. By 15 April the Afrika Korps were in a position to assault Tobruk, and had pushed on to take the Halfaya Pass.

Worse still, O'Connor, Lieutenant-General Philip Neame, OC of Allied and Commonwealth Forces in Cyrenaica, and Major-General Michael

Gambier-Parry, commander of the 2nd Armoured Division, were captured by a German patrol on April 6th, a circumstance which gives some idea of the fluidity and speed of operations in the desert. Gambier-Parry's unit had also been effectively destroyed in the German advance on Tobruk.

After the repulse of three attacks on Tobruk (which was defended by some 25,000 Allied troops, many of them from the 9th Australian Division), Rommel laid siege to the port. In the meantime on 15 and 16 May, the Allies counterattacked. Operation Brevity, conducted in three columns, was designed to inflict as much damage as possible on the Axis forces and reclaim the Halfaya Pass. It achieved the last objective, but a German counterattack on the 16th forced the British back, with significant losses. The Allies held the Halfaya Pass only until the Afrika Korps launched Unternehmen Skorpion (Operation Scorpion) to take it back on 26 May.

The next significant Allied gambit was Operation Battleaxe, the main intention of which was to lift the siege of Tobruk and win back lost ground in eastern Cyrenaica. The arrival of Tiger Convoy in Alexandria on 12 May brought the Allies much-needed armoured reinforcements, but the tanks which arrived needed to be unloaded, adapted to desert conditions and brought up to the front, which all took a month.

Further delay resulted from the needs of 7th Armoured Division to familiarize itself with its new equipment. The operation finally kicked off on 15 June with a three-phase plan: the area around Halfaya Pass was to be secured, then XIII Corps was to capture the area around Tobruk. Finally, Derna and Mechili were to be taken.

Despite successful softening up by the RAF, Battleaxe ran into early problems due to faulty intelligence. The German armour was not concentrated where the Allies believed it would be, and the assault on Halfaya Pass failed. A German counterattack was contained, but on 17 June the Allies were threatened with an encircling manoeuvre by two Panzer regiments, and were forced to extract themselves. They suffered close to 1,000 casualties and lost 98 tanks, while making only relatively insignificant local gains.

Churchill's response to the failure of Battleaxe was brisk. Wavell was replaced by General Claude Auchinleck, and Major General O'Moore Creagh, commander of the 7th Armoured Division, was also relieved. The

Western Desert Force, now under the command of Lieutenant-General Alan Cunningham, was renamed the Eighth Army.

The Allies next attempt to relieve Tobruk and roll back German gains in Libya met with more success; this was Operation Crusader. The concept of Crusader was to engage and destroy the Afrika Korp's armour, using the 7th Armoured Division. On their right, XIII Corps would move to outflank German positions and threaten the German rear. Meanwhile, XXX would push on to Tobruk to relieve the siege.

Crusader began on 18 November, and initially caught the Axis troops unawares (Rommel was actually out of the country, so sure was he that no Allied assault was imminent). In fierce fighting in all the main areas of the attack, lasting for over a month, the Allies secured their key objectives, but at a fearsome cost, particularly in armour. At the Battle of Sidi Rezegh, in particular, the 7th Armoured Division suffered crippling losses when engaging the German armour, and was deemed to have performed so poorly that Auchinleck replaced its commander, Cunningham, with Lieutenant General Neil Ritchie, a more aggressive option. Operation Crusader was particularly notable for the speed at which tactical situations developed and changed at various points in the operation, and for several outstandingly courageous actions fought by troops who were caught up in the maelstrom. The battle also showed that German armoured forces could be defeated, although there is little doubt that tactically they had the upper hand; as ever in the desert, the most implacable enemy was the logistical situation.

By the end of 1941 the key port of Tobruk was back in Allied hands, with the Axis forces having retired westwards to El Agheila. Now, however, the pendulum swung back in Rommel's favour. It was the Allies' turn to be overstretched. Early 1942 would see Rommel's Axis forces at their most effective.

With the expansion and renaming of the Axis forces in North Africa to Panzerarmee Afrika in January came a commensurate flexing of muscle. In Unternehmen Theseus (Operation Theseus), beginning on 21 January, the Panzerarmee defeated the 2nd Armoured Brigade, halving its armoured strength, and retook Benghazi on 28 January, subsequently pushing the British back to the line of fortifications at Gazala in early February. After lengthy preparations, Rommel launched a flanking attack round the Gazala line in May, but his mixed German and Italian force became cut off by Free French forces near Bir Hakeim. Having retreated, Rommel then withstood an Allied counterattack, codenamed Operation Aberdeen, and turned the situation brilliantly to his advantage, inflicting heavy losses on 22 Armoured Brigade and cutting off the 9th Indian Brigade. The Allies were forced to retreat rapidly from the Gazala line in mid-June. By 21 June, Tobruk was back in Axis hands, with the disastrous loss of 35,000 Allied prisoners, and despite the fact that Auchinleck had believed that it could hold out for some time. In fact, the garrison surrendered in a day. Now Rommel had a relatively accessible port from which to supply his forces. Auchinleck subsequently relieved Ritchie of his post, although this was unrelated to the loss of Tobruk, and took personal command of the Eighth Army.

The catalogue of Allied calamities continued. Panzerarmee Afrika drove on into Egypt and closed in on the British base at Mersa Matruh, where the Axis forces were again victorious in an action fought between 26 and 29 June, 1942. Rommel set out to defeat the retreating Eighth Army in detail, and before they could establish a fortified defensive line. Despite the growing effectiveness of the Allied Desert Air Force, and serious losses inflicted on Rommel's signals capability at the Battle of Gazala, Rommel was able to press home the attack, largely owing to command confusion on the Allied side which led XIII Corps to retreat from Mersa Matruh leaving X Corps stranded. This occurred at a point in the battle when a decisive attack on the 90th Light Division could have swung the battle the other way. In more often-confused fighting, the Allies were able to withdraw most of their men, with elements of X Corps, notably the 2nd New Zealand Division, having to fight their way out of an encirclement. However, Rommel was still able to take more than 6,000 prisoners, and sent the 90th Light Division on down the coastal road to pursue the fleeing Eighth Army. Panzerarmee captured large quantities of stores.

July 1942 began with the Allied forces pushed right back to El Alamein, little more than 60 miles from Alexandria. In Alexandria and Cairo, the atmosphere was panicky. The Suez Canal and the great Egyptian ports were under direct threat. At this point, however, Rommel was finally halted. Throughout July, in what would become known as the First Battle of El Alamein, Panzerarmee Afrika tried and failed to dislodge the Eighth Army from its defensive positions.

Rommel was prevented from attempting a wide southwards outflanking manoeuvre by the presence to the south of El Alamein of the Qattara Depression, a low lying area of impassable sand dunes and salt marshes. He therefore attempted to force his way through perceived gaps in the Allied lines and send the 90th Light Division north to cut the coastal road, the main line of eastward retreat, while despatching the 15th and 21st Panzer divisions south to attack the rear of XIII Corps. Both thrusts would be supported by Italian divisions. In the event, the attacks became bogged down by determined defence and the southern sweep of the Panzer divisions was called off, with the formations being reassigned to help 90th Division in its push north. Allied counterattacks in the area of Ruweisat Ridge also severely hampered Axis operations. As the battle progressed, the growing Allied superiority in materiel began to tell. The Axis troops, including large numbers of Italians in the centre of the line, were suffering badly from lack of manpower, armour and fuel. By 27 July both sides had acknowledged a stalemate, despite a series of attacks and counterattacks from both sides. German losses were about 10,000 men, plus an unknown number of Italians and 7,000 prisoners. The Eighth Army suffered over 13,000 casualties.

In the aftermath of the battle, Churchill chose to replace Auchinleck. He brought in General Sir Harold Alexander as C-in-C Middle East, and initially appointed the commander of XIII Corps, Lieutenant-General William Gott to the command of Eighth Army. Gott, however was killed on 7th August when the plane he was travelling on, en route to take up his command, was shot down. His replacement, who took up command on 13 August, was Lieutenant-General Bernard Montgomery.

Montgomery's first task was to deal with an attempt, carried out between 30 August and 5 September, to envelop Eighth Army and drive for Cairo. At the Battle of Alam el Halfa, the attempt, undertaken by understrength and battle weary Axis troops, was beaten off.

With greatly shortened supply lines and an increase in the quality of arms arriving, Montgomery was able to execute his plan to build up a decisive superiority in resources over his Axis opponents, who were struggling with exhaustion, illness, lack of fuel and vehicles, and the inability to replenish what they had. The Allied troops, by contrast, had regrouped and were in good spirits. At the outset of what would become known as the Second Battle of El Alamein (or just 'El Alamein'), Allied forces enjoyed a superiority in men and tanks of close to 2:1, with perhaps 195,000 men to Rommel's 100,000, of whom well under half were front-line ready. The Allies had also taken delivery of many more of the American M4 Sherman tanks, which were a significant upgrade on those British tanks they had been using.

The offensive opened on 23 October and within a week attrition had brought the Axis forces to a critical state. Despite enjoying the same advantages that the Allies had when defending El Alamein (the secured southern flank chief amongst them), the Panzerarmee was hampered by its lack of resources, and by the fact the Allies, by means of Ultra decrypts, had a clear idea of Axis dispositions and strength. Ultra decrypts had also allowed the Allies to restrict Axis resupply by targeting Mediterranean convoys. The Panzerarmee also lost Rommel's deputy, General Georg Stumme, to a heart attack while Rommel himself was absent in Germany. Even so, and despite the fact that they realized that the Germans would not be able to fight their usual wide-ranging and fluid tactics, the Allies underestimated the resilience of the defence. After more than a week of heavy fighting, during which the Allies had cleared paths through Axis minefields and brought severe pressure to bear on the Axis lines, and during which the Axis had also scored some tactical victories, it became clear to Rommel that his situation was not tenable. On 3 November, Rommel informed the Army High Command of his decision to retreat. The response was an order from Hitler to hold their positions to the last man. Rommel, shocked by the order, initially complied, but finally ordered a retreat on 4 November, prioritizing the motorized units. By the time news came through that Hitler had changed his mind, it was too late to save the infantry formations.

As what remained of Panzerarmee Afrika began a chaotic retreat, the British and Americans launched Operation Torch, a series of seaborne and airborne landings in Morocco with the agreement of local, nominally Vichy-controlled French government forces. Military operations commenced on 8 November. The intended outcome was to open a second front within Africa and to finish off the Axis presence there.

The immediate consequence for Rommel was that resupply which might have been on its way to his forces was now diverted to oppose Operation Torch. Panzerarmee Afrika fought a delaying action at El Agheila in December which allowed the remnants of the Axis forces to escape capture by the Eighth Army, but the pursuit and attacks from the air meant that the constant problems of attrition were exacerbated. As the Panzerarmee Afrika retreated across Libya towards Tunisia, giving up en route Tobruk and Benghazi, it became clear that the end could not be long delayed. Although there was an Axis presence in Tunisia, the Armeegruppe Afrika under Generaloberst von Arnim was fully occupied fighting the British First Army and their American allies in the aftermath of Operation Torch.

On 23 January 1943, Allied forces took Tripoli, which had been Panzerarmee's last viable port of supply in Libya. Rommel's intent at this point was to retire to a defensive point in Tunisia, the Gabès Gap. However, while the strategy was probably the only realistic one open to him, it did free up an enormous amount of territory of which the Allies could make use, particularly from the point of view of resupply, and the establishment of forward air bases. His memoirs record his surprise and anger at the arrival in Tunisia of reinforcements that could have made a crucial difference had they been available to him at the time of the battles of El Alamein.

The last hurrah of Panzerarmee Afrika came at the Battle of the Kasserine Pass between 19 and 24 February, the first substantial combat encounter between American and German forces in the Second World War. The result was a stinging reverse for the American II Corps, whose combat inexperience led them to make a string of errors in opposing a determined German attack, blundering into a carefully prepared series of anti-tank positions. The battle confirmed the bulk of Tunisia under Axis control, but strategically, there was little value to that. With the Eighth Army, freshly resupplied, advancing from the east, and the First Army, strengthened in the aftermath of Torch and advancing from the west, Axis forces in North

Africa were forced to surrender on 13 May 1943, giving up more than 250,000 prisoners of war.

For Hitler and Germany, the war in the desert had been little more than a sideshow when set against the overwhelming importance of the build up and execution of Barbarossa against the Russians. For the Allies, however, its final outcome was a hugely important boost to morale. The Axis war machine could be beaten, and with the entry of America into the war at the end of 1941, the upswing in public mood following the Second Battle of El Alamein carried through to the more significant triumphs of the later war.

Chapter Two

Armies, Organization, and Equipment

The Desert War was fought across a transitional period of the Second World War, battled out between decidedly weak, inter-war equipment and tactics to begin with, but evolving into a far more sophisticated method of combined arms warfare by the end of the period.

In broad terms, the Desert War was fought in several distinct phases:

- Phase 1: British & Commonwealth versus Italian forces (1940–1).
- Phase 2: British & Commonwealth versus Italian and German forces (1941–2).
- Phase 3: American and British & Commonwealth versus German and Italian forces (1942–3).

The main combatants throughout the North African campaign included the British and Italians, the Germans, and later the Americans. In addition, a wide and wonderful number of other nationalities were represented from around Britain's empire (Australians, New Zealanders, South Africans, and Indians especially), and also the troops of Vichy and Free France, Polish units equipped by British and American allies, and locally-raised units. It's perfectly acceptable to field only 'middle of the road' troops in their generic desert kit, but also great fun to raise your own units from some of the more exotic choices – the Libyan Division of the Italian army, serving in an 'askari' style uniform; British troops wearing US uniforms taking part in the Operation Torch landings, in the belief that the Vichy French would more likely surrender to Americans (suggested by Churchill, although it's unclear if this ever actually happened in any of the landings); Senegalese infantry under Vichy French command; the British 3rd Hussars or 6th RTR in captured Italian M13/40 tanks after Beda Fomm; and so on.

Organization

Inevitably, the wargame rules you choose will generally provide their own organizational structure for your armies in the game, rather than expecting you to convert your knowledge of the forces involved into suitable forces in play. However, if you do wish to look in more detail at the historical make-up of the Desert War armies, the following books are a good starting point, as are accounts of individual operations detailing which units fought where (and when, as this sometimes changed between years):

- *Osprey Battle Orders 20: Rommel's Afrika Korps* (Pier Paolo Battistelli).
- *Osprey Battle Orders 21: US Armored Units in the North African and Italian Campaigns 1942–45* (Steven J Zaloga).
- *Osprey Battle Orders 23: Desert Raiders, Axis and Allied Special Forces 1940–43* (Andrea Molinari).
- *Osprey Battle Orders 28: Desert Rats* (Tim Moreman).

I'd also suggest looking at the *Flames of War* 'intelligence handbooks' and *Rapid Fire!* supplements discussed in Chapter Four for smaller unit organizations from a wargaming perspective. Even if you do not play the *Flames of War* rules, the breakdown of units into gaming proportions and types of equipment is a valuable guide. Another resource worth referring to for the organization of forces – across all theatres of the Second World War – is the excellent Bayonet Strength website (online search: 'bayonet strength 150 ww2').

However, it is of course worthwhile to include *some* detail of the way units were organized, to give players a prompt to start collecting broadly historical and balanced forces, and to assist those whose rules of choice are less than prescriptive about the forces each player should field.

The higher level, divisional organization of both Allied and Axis armies in the Desert War were not too dissimilar. In fact, the one unifying characteristic of all forces in the Desert War was fluidity – units would come and go from battlegroups; they would be combined with other (understrength) units to form a new strike force; they would be underequipped and undermanned (especially in the early part of the campaign); and above all else, each divisional, brigade, or lower-level commander would be expected to 'do one's best with the resources available'. It's worth noting that British nomenclature differed slightly from other armies, just to add an additional layer of confusion. I can imagine what you are thinking, and yes, to some extent fielding a force for the Desert War does pretty much allow you to choose the equipment and formations you fancy fielding (within the realms of historical plausibility), rather than being tied to very rigid organization charts. The Desert War would have been a Corporate HR team's worst nightmare.

In general terms, on paper, formations were organized as shown below. The reality, as noted earlier, was often rather different and depended on battle and campaign attrition, meaning that some formations functioned with a very different strength to those shown. The structure of various formations also altered over the course of the Desert War, so the lists below are simplified guidelines to give some basic structure to your model collection. Artillery, anti-tank, anti-aircraft, medium machinegun, recon and other supporting units were usually added from divisional resources to the brigade-level formations. A division generally consisted of three infantry or armoured regiments plus the support units.

Britain
- Infantry Brigade » 3 battalions.
- Battalion » 4 rifle companies plus support platoons.
- Rifle company » 3 platoons.
- Platoon » 3 rifle sections.
- Rifle section » 10 men.

- Armoured Brigade » 3 armoured regiments, 1 motorized infantry battalion.
- Armoured Regiment » 3 squadrons.
- Squadron » 5 troops.
- Troop » 3 or 4 tanks.

Germany
- Panzergrenadier regiment » 2 battalions.
- Battalion » 3 rifle companies, 1 heavy weapons company.
- Rifle company » 3 platoons.
- Platoon » 3 rifle squads.
- Squad » 14 men.

- Panzer regiment » 2 panzer battalions.
- Battalion » 2 light companies, 1 medium company.
- Company » 4 platoons.
- Platoon » 5 tanks.

Italy
- Infantry regiment » 3 battalions plus support companies.
- Battalion » 3 rifle companies.
- Rifle company » 3 platoons.
- Platoon » 2 squads.
- Squad » 20 men.

US
- Infantry regiment » 3 battalions.
- Battalion » 3 rifle companies, 1 heavy weapons company.
- Rifle company » 3 platoons.
- Platoon » 3 rifle sections.
- Rifle section » 12 men.

- Armored regiment » 1 light battalion, 2 medium battalions.
- Battalion » 3 companies.
- Company » 3 platoons.
- Platoon » 5 tanks.

Equipment

Most sets of rules provide very detailed breakdowns of the equipment available to each army in bespoke army lists (sometimes including very specific dates of use), and the relative merits of said equipment within that particular rules set. Being a subjective value, certain rules award quirks or bonuses to certain equipment not noted in other rules.

A comprehensive listing of all marques of vehicle, calibres of guns, and variations in infantry weapons are best left on the pages of books specifically considering such materiel. The following tables therefore provide useful data on commonly acquired models and equipment that will be of use if you're writing your own rules or need to tweak a pre-existing set (for example if your rules have no specific data for Desert War units).

Remember that equipment continued to be used until units received a refit, meaning that its effectiveness would decline the further removed in time from its introduction – a good example of this is the British Matilda II tank, which quickly emerged as 'Queen of the Battlefield' early in the campaign when it was pretty much impervious to enemy anti-tank weapons, but degraded in effectiveness (and protective value) towards the end of its lengthy frontline service. Similarly, the infamous British 2pdr antitank gun began the campaign as an adequate weapon against contemporary enemy tanks, but remained in service with infantry units well beyond its ability to penetrate first-rate German armour. This should certainly be borne in mind when collecting and equipping your units.

Tanks of the Desert War

AFV	Nation	Armament	Max. armour (mm)	Top speed mph (road / cross-country)	Crew	Range (miles)	Notes
Light Mk VI	Britain	1 x HMG, 1x MG	14	35 / 25	3	130	Poor performance when used as battle tank.
Matilda II	Britain	2pdr, 1x MG	78	15 / 8	4	70	Heavily armoured; dominated until German tanks upgunned. Known as 'The Queen of the Desert'.
Valentine	Britain	2pdr (later 6pdr), 1x MG	65	15 / 8	3 (later 4)	90	Replacement for Matilda II infantry tank; less heavily armoured but capable of being upgunned.
Churchill	Britain	6pdr, 2x MG	102	15 / 8	5	56	75mm main gun was introduced in Tunisia.
A9	Britain	2pdr, 3x MG	14	25 / 15	6	100	Mechanically unreliable.
A10	Britain	2pdr, 2x MG	30	16 / 8	5	100	'Heavy' cruiser; mechanically unreliable.
A13 Mk II	Britain	2pdr, 1x MG	30	30 / 14	4	90	Best of the British 'A' number cruisers.

AFV	Nation	Armament	Max. armour (mm)	Top speed mph (road / cross-country)	Crew	Range (miles)	Notes
Crusader	Britain	2pdr (later 6pdr), 1x MG (2x on Crusader I)	40 (later 51)	27 / 15	5 (later 3)	100	First British tank truly capable of being upgraded with additional armour and heavier gun. Early marques mechanically unreliable.
Panzer I	Germany	2x MG	13	23 / 12	2	95	Used mostly as command vehicle and also as chassis for self-propelled guns.
Panzer II	Germany	20mm, 1x MG	30	35 / 12	3	77	Better performance when used for recon and flanking actions.
Panzer III	Germany	50mm (D marque, 37mm; J marque, long barrel), 2x MG	30	25 / 11	5	102	37mm gun limited to early campaign; later marques up-armoured 'long barrel' or 'special' 50mm gun introduced on Panzer III J.
Panzer IV	Germany	75mm (F1, short barrel; F2, long barrel), 2x MG	50	26 / 13	5	125	'Long barrel' or 'special' 75mm gun introduced on Panzer IV F2.
Tiger	Germany	88mm, 2 MG	100	28 / 14	5	120	Used in Tunisia in very limited numbers.

Name	Country	Armament	Armour	Speed	Crew	No.	Notes
CV 3/35 (also L3–35)	Italy	2x MG (sometimes flamethrower)	14	26 / 12	2	78	In the words of Rommel: 'completely obsolete design'. Poor performance and mechanically unreliable.
L6/40	Italy	20mm, 1x MG	40	26 / 12	2	120	Good light tank, but obsolete before introduction in later part of campaign.
M11/39	Italy	47mm, 3x MG	30	19 / 8	3	125	Poor performance and mechanically unreliable. Hull mounted 47mm gun with MGs in turret; unable to fire from hull-down position.
M13/40	Italy	47mm, 3x MG	30	19 / 8	4	125	Mechanically unreliable. Also M14/41 with upgraded engine but similar performance.
Stuart	US	37mm, 3x MG	38	36 / 20	4	70	Also used by UK, where it was known as a Honey.
Lee / Grant	US	75mm in hull, 37mm in turret, 3–4x MG	50	26 / 16	6	120	Also used by UK, and first Allied tank to outgun German AFVs. Couldn't fight hull-down due to 75mm's placement. Minor spec differences between US Lee model and British Grant model. Introduced at Battle of Gazala.
Sherman	US	75mm, 2x MG	50	24 / 15	5	100	Also used by UK, and introduced at Second El Alamein.

Rifles of the Desert War

Rifle	Nation	Calibre	Rate of fire*	Magazine capacity	Muzzle velocity	Effective range*	Notes
Lee-Enfield (SMLE No 4)	Britain	7.7mm	18–20 rounds per minute	10 rounds	744 m/s	500 m	Bolt action.
Mauser Karabiner 98k (Kar 98k)	Germany	7.92mm	15 rounds per minute	5 rounds	7.60 m/s	500 m	Bolt action.
Carcano (M91)	Italy	6.5mm or 7.35mm	15 rounds per minute	6 rounds	700 m/s	300 m	Bolt action.
Garand (M1)	US	7.62mm	16–24 rounds per minute (Semi-auto)	8 rounds	853 m/s	450 m	Semi-automatic; often allowed to move & fire in wargame rules due to this.

* Rates of fire and ranges are often disputed or subject to widely varying factors and numbers, but those shown above give a reasonable comparison between weapons. For SMGs and MGs, the noted rate of fire is cyclical rather than a combat statistic.

Anti-tank Guns of the Desert War

Gun	Nation	Effective range / Armour penetration	Maximum range / Armour penetration	Notes
2 pdr (40mm)	Britain	500m / 57mm	1,000 / 45mm	Standard British tank gun up to 1942. No HE.
6 pdr (57mm)	Britain	500m / 90mm	1,000 / 74mm	Introduced at Gazala, 1942. Mounted in Crusader III and later British tanks. Poor HE – crews recorded as using MGs in preference.
20mm KwK 30	Germany	500m / 21mm	–	Mounted on Panzer II.
37mm KwK	Germany	500m / 35mm	–	Mounted on earliest versions of Panzer III; rare in Desert War.
50mm KwK (short barrel)	Germany	750m / 45mm	1,000m / 30mm	Mounted in Panzer III E – H.
50mm KwK 39 (long barrel)	Germany	750m / 54mm	1,000m / 45mm	Panzer III J onwards. Known to the British as a 'Special'.
75mm KwK KwK 37 (short barrel)	Germany	500m / 40mm	–	Mounted in Panzer IV F1; better suited to infantry howitzer role.
75mm KwK 40 (long barrel)	Germany	750m / 85mm	1,500m / 60mm	Mounted in Panzer IV F2. Known to the British as a 'Special'.
88mm Flak 18/36	Germany	1,250m / 95mm	2,000m / 65mm	The infamous 'eighty-eight' anti-aircraft gun, used as ATG.

Gun	Nation	Effective range / Armour penetration	Maximum range / Armour penetration	Notes
88mm KwK 36	Germany	1,500 / 95mm	2,000m / 70mm	Mounted in Tiger I.
37mm 37/45	Italy	500m / 48mm	750m / 41mm	Infantry ATG.
47mm M1932/42	Italy	500m / 43mm	-	Mounted in M13/40 and M14/41 tanks.
37mm M6	US	500m / 61mm	1,000m / 40mm	Mounted In M3 Stuart and M3 Lee/Grant (turret)
57mm M1	US	500m / 100mm	1,000m / 73mm	Infantry ATG.
75mm M3	US	500m / 70mm	1,000m / 45mm	Mounted in M3 Lee/Grant (hull) and M4 Sherman. Better performance as HE weapon.
76mm M7	US	1,000m / 80mm	1,500m / 60mm	Mounted in M10 tank destroyer.

Self-propelled Guns and Tank Destroyers of the Desert War

AFV	Nation	Armament	Top Speed mph (road / cross-country)	Crew
Bishop	Britain	25pdr	15	3
Deacon	Britain	6pdr	19	4
Marder Sdkfz 139	Germany	76mm	26	4
Panzerjäger I	Germany	47mm	25	3
Semovente 75/18	Italy	75mm	20	3
Semovente 47/32	Italy	47mm	26	3
T12 / M3 GMC	US	75mm	47	5
M7 Priest	US	105mm	25	7

Submachine Guns in the Desert War

SMG	Nation	Calibre	Rate of fire*	Magazine capacity	Muzzle velocity	Effective range*
Sten	Britain	9mm	500 rpm	32	365 m/s	100m
MP40 'Schmeisser'	Germany	9mm	500–500 rpm	32	400 m/s	100m
Berretta 38	Italy	9mm	600 rpm	10–30	429 m/s	100m
Thompson	US	0.45"	600–725 rpm	20–30	285 m/s	100m

* Rates of fire and ranges are often disputed or subject to widely varying factors and numbers, but those shown above give a reasonable comparison between weapons. For SMGs and MGs, the noted rate of fire is cyclical rather than a combat statistic.

Light, Medium & Heavy Machine-guns of the Desert War

MG	Nation	Calibre	Rate of fire*	Magazine capacity	Muzzle velocity	Effective range*	Role
Bren	Britain	0.303″	500–520 rpm	30	744 m/s	550m	Squad LMG
Vickers	Britain	0.303″	450–500 rpm	250 round belt	744 m/s	2,000m	MMG
MG34	Germany	7.92mm	800–900 rpm	50 or 75 / 250 round belt	765 m/s	1,200m	Squad LMG & MMG
MG42	Germany	7.92mm	1,200 rpm	50 / 250 round belt	740 m/s	2,000m	Squad LMG & MMG
Breda 30	Italy	6.5mm	500 rpm	20	620 m/s	1,000m	Squad LMG
M1918 BAR	US	0.30-06″	300–500 rpm	20	860 m/s	1,300m	Squad LMG
M1919 Browning	US	0.30-06″	400–600 rpm	250 round belt	850 m/s	1,400m	HMG

* Rates of fire and ranges are often disputed or subject to widely varying factors and numbers, but those shown above give a reasonable comparison between weapons. For SMGs and MGs, the noted rate of fire is cyclical rather than a combat statistic.

Painting your armies

Painters who fret over getting the exact shades of paint 'correct' on their models can take a breather when assembling Desert War forces. The effect of sand weathering and heat bleaching on clothing, equipment, and vehicles meant that there was little uniformity on either side. German uniforms were notorious for bleaching to a variety of shades from sand to brown, while camouflage on AFVs varied according to the quartermaster's paint supply and the number of sand storms a vehicle had been subjected to. Fielding a rag-tag bunch of models seems wholly realistic for this campaign – although to add some uniformity, I recommend finishing all of a force's bases using the same colour scheme, to prevent your proud force from looking like a travelling circus. The hobby being what it is, it's also fine to present a perfectly uniform, neat and tidy desert force. Should 'that type of wargamer' question your perfectly matched troops and platoons, inform them that your force has just been freshly refitted, and is ready for action.

I am not the kind of painter who should dispense arcane or award-winning painting advice; so I rarely discuss actual painting techniques. This is for the general good of miniatures gaming. However, to achieve reasonable 'wargaming standard' units for the Desert War, I've found three relatively simple and quick to use methods to be very useful. They are already recognized and popular techniques, but truly come into their own when painting so many models in light sand colours:

- **'The wash' on infantry:** This is a simple painting technique that gets your models painted quickly and looking acceptable on the tabletop – under close scrutiny they'll win no awards, but in a game they'll perform just as well as the winners of those awards! Paint your models in whatever base colour you've chosen for uniforms (see later for ideas); cover all of the model, so don't leave faces, rifles, equipment and so on uncovered. Leave it to dry; don't watch this, I hear it's very boring. Once fully dried, dilute some mid-brown paint or buy a purpose made 'wash' or 'ink' for modellers. Paint this over the entire model – faces, weapons, and all. This thin wash emphasizes the model's sculpting, flowing into creases and hollows to create a shaded effect. Once dried, I then quickly fill in faces, paint weapons, and use a second colour to highlight equipment – all the time, leaving the shadow of the wash intact (for example, I'll paint cheeks, chin, nose and brow on a face, but the recesses of the face are left the colour of the wash). At this stage you can add as much or as little extra detail as you wish. Once dried, I cover the model in a matt varnish, as the wash has a tendency to dry with a glossy sheen. As noted above, you will win no painting awards with this method, but it is an efficient way to bring your fully painted force to the table swiftly.

- **Black-lining on AFVs:** Without some extra work, a horde of Desert War AFVs look distinctly vanilla – in more ways than one, as you'll see naught but a sea of sandy-yellow before you. Well sculpted models can rise above this, but some subtly rendered definition of shape and detail will make your AFVs stand out better on the tabletop. With a bit of experience, the 'wash' technique described previously can be used with some success especially on 10mm and 6mm models, but must be painted on with a light touch – otherwise the watered down paint or ink tends to pool on the flat surface of your AFV, which definitely is not a finish you'll want! (It can be rescued by carefully painting over the flat surfaces after applying the wash.) A commonly used technique over the past few years has been to 'black line' AFVs. This is essentially as it sounds: around the edges of hatches, running gear, and so on, a very thin black line stands out from the sandy base colour, adding definition. The best way to achieve this is to undercoat your AFV with black paint. Once this has dried, 'fill in' the sandy base colour over it, leaving a fine black line against all encountered edges. Depending on the tone chosen for your model, you may need to paint several layers to stop the black undercoat making everything seem too dark. This is a fairly simple technique to master, but the real skill comes in knowing how much black to leave on show – it's easy to overdo it, leaving your model looking like one of Picasso's early – and unsuccessful – experiments in Cubism.
- **Basing:** Many experienced wargamers will tell you that an average paint job with a well-finished base looks much better than a great paint job with a shoddy base. And they're right. Using the two

techniques described above gives you a finished force of reasonable paint quality. But where they'll come into their own is through the basing. Whatever method you choose, spend some time making it look good. I recommend waiting until all of your force is finished and then tackling the bases all at the same time – this gives a consistent finish that helps to 'bind' them together as a cohesive force. As with the models themselves, you'll be using a very sandy-coloured palette for Desert War bases. My own method is to paint a thick, slightly lumpy chocolate brown base layer (don't get this on the tracks or legs of models!). As this is drying, I sprinkle on some sand or fine modeller's gravel to add some extra texture. Leave it to dry... be patient! Over this, I paint a fairly heavy layer of dark sand, covering all of the base except for any 'shadow' left under the sand/gravel. Again, leave to dry... and again be patient! The next step is to drybrush a lighter shade of sand over the surface (something approximating the main colour of your models works well); done correctly, this will emphasize the textures of the base. Once this has dried, I make a few small highlights with an even lighter shade to pick out detail. The end step is to add a few stingy clumps of grass or scrub to a few bases – I position this so that all bases in the same unit have a similar pattern, to help to identify them mid battle. An excellent online tutorial for theming your bases to different North African regions is available on the *Flames of War* website, created by the serendipitously named Jeremy Painter (online search: 'jeremy painter desert basing').

As a general guide to start you getting your paint brushes wet, I recommend following the chart below when painting your models; as noted above, variation is absolutely acceptable – and accurate. I've included the codes I use based on the popular Vallejo Model Color range, which are commonly used by Second World War modellers. Jean Restayn's *WWII Tank Encyclopedia in Color 1939–45* (2007) is a good reference book for AFV colour schemes.

Plenty of tips and colour swatches are available online, helping you to be more selective in the tones you're looking for, and being more prescriptive as to precise AFV painting methods (online search: 'WW2 desert painting guide'). Some paint manufacturers now list in their ranges specific colour sets for each of the main nations involved in the Desert War.

Infantry	Colour	Vallejo Model Color
British uniform	Sand	Iraqi Sand 819 or Dark Sand 847
British webbing & kit	Light khaki	Stone Grey 884 or German Camo Beige 821
German uniform	Khaki green through to sand	Russian Uniform 924, US Field Drab 873, Iraqi Sand 819 or Flat Earth 983
German webbing & kit	Sand & leather	Iraqi Sand 819 & Mahogany Brown 846
Italian uniform	Sand	Dark Sand 847 or Desert Yellow 977
Italian webbing & kit	Light khaki & leather	Yellow Green 881 & Mahogany Brown 846
American uniform	Jacket: Olive Trousers: Khaki	Jacket: Brown Violet 887 Trousers: US Field Drab 873
American webbing & kit	Khaki green	Green Grey 886

AFVs	Colour	Vallejo Model Color
British Western Desert base layer	Light stone	Dark Sand 847 or Iraqi Sand 819
British Tunisia base layer (First Army, shipped direct from UK)	Khaki brown	Khaki Grey 880
British camouflage	Dark brown, dark green or black	German Camo Medium Brown 826, Bronze Green 897 or German Grey 995 / Black 950
German base layer	Dark sand	Iraqi Sand 819

AFVs	Colour	Vallejo Model Color
Italian base layer	Sand or olive green grey	Green Ochre 914 or German Fieldgrey 830
Italian camouflage	Dark green	Olive Grey 888
American base layer	Olive green grey or sand	Brown Violet 887 or Dark Sand 847

British AFV camouflage

Most Desert War AFVs should be finished in one of countless shades of 'sand' or the olive shades of some American and Italian vehicles. Tales of early Afrika Korps panzers remaining in their European grey finish may be found, although it's not entirely clear whether this scheme ever appeared on the frontline. But for real variety, it is the usually sartorially conservative British army that brings a dash of (dowdy) colour to the desert.

A number of different AFV camouflage schemes were used by the British over time, and given the weathering effect of the desert on paintwork, there's more scope than usual for a whole palette of colour variation, including:

- **1940:** Overall sand (variation throughout the campaign from a yellow–cream to pink–brown depending on paint stocks and weathering).
- **1940–41:** Splinter or Caunter scheme: opinion varies on the specific colours (and is, from time to time, enthusiastically debated by wargamers and military modellers), but essentially this was a three-tone angular, fan-like pattern radiating from the front hull towards the rear of the tank. Colours shown for this pattern vary from light blue through to dark grey and purple–brown, including a variety of light and mid greys: light stone (sand), silver grey (light green–grey), and slate (dark green-grey) are commonly referred to. A two-colour variant was intended for use in Sudan, but some of the cruiser tanks painted in this way ended up serving in the Western Desert (with angular patches of purple-brown over the standard light stone). My tip for painting Caunter schemes is to use modeller's masking tape to achieve a straight line – without this, it's harder than you might think to paint a straight line!

- **1942–43:** Irregular stripes and patches similar to the patterns used by the RAF on aircraft. A lighter, sand colour usually provided the under-layer (a darker colour was used in Tunisia by the British First Army as these units had shipped from the UK), with irregular patches of dark brown or black being applied over the top. Again, variations existed either by design or weathering, so that the darker colour sometimes appeared green or grey. The top decking of AFVs was often left in plain sand on Crusader tanks; the distinctive wheels of the Crusader also sometimes had the middle three of them painted black, possibly to give the appearance of a truck at distance – this latter pattern being unique to the Eighth Army.

Barry Beldam's superb Armoured Acorn website is a great reference when painting the many and varied tones of British camouflage, including detailed illustrations of individual AFVs' patterns, plus tactical markings. (online search: 'armoured acorn AFV').

AFV tactical markings

Almost all AFVs in the Desert War carried a number of distinctive markings on them to identify themselves, more to their friends than their enemies. It's perfectly acceptable from a wargamer's perspective to ignore such additional artwork, allowing your generically painted AFVs to serve in any unit of your choice, but I can assure you that adding a few markings over the top of your sandy paint job really brings your models to life. And rather than relying on freehand painting skills, suitable decals are available for models in 15mm, 20mm, and 28mm.

Aside from divisional markings such as the famous 'desert rat' of the British 7th Armoured Division, the rhino of the British 1st Armoured Division, or the red bull's head of the American 34th Division, many vehicles carried national insignia. For the Germans this was the *balkenkreuz* (a cross) – either black or without colour, bordered white; and for the Americans it was a five-pointed star, which was usually white or yellow with no background colour, but sometimes white in a blue circle (the outlining white circle so well-known from D-Day onwards did not appear until July

1943, after the end of the Desert War). Free French forces used a *tricolore* alongside other markings. British AFVs carried no national flag, instead sometimes using three vertical bars of colour: white–red–white early in the campaign (for Operation Crusader), changing to red–white–red before the First Army's arrival in Tunisia. National markings were painted on the sides of AFVs, or on the turret; national flags (or for the British, roundels), were occasionally placed on decking for aerial identification. Reused captured AFVs prominently displayed symbols and colours to make things clear which side they were fighting for!

Alongside these, individual companies and platoons had their own markings on turrets:

- **Germany** used a series of three-digit identification numbers based on 'company – troop – tank in troop': 101 was the 1st company's commander; 111 was the troop leader of the 1st troop, 1st company; 131 was the troop leader of the 3rd troop, 1st company; 301 was the 3rd company's commander' 645 was the fifth tank, 4th troop, 6th company; and so on. Colours were either red or black with a white outline. Confusingly, a number of inconsistencies exist, but the above explanation is accurate enough when applying decals to AFVs.
- **Italy** used coloured blocks and bars: red for the 1st company, pale blue for the 2nd, yellow for the 3rd, green for the 4th, black for battalion HQ, and white for regimental HQ. The first platoon's tanks carried two bars, the second platoon three bars, and so on; company commanders used a solid block.
- **Britain** used coloured, hollow geometric shapes: senior battalion/ regiment used red; 2nd battalion/regiment used yellow; junior battalion/ regiment used blue. Within each, the HQ used a hollow diamond; A Squadron used a hollow triangle; B Squadron used a hollow square; C Squadron used a hollow circle.
- **America** employed a series of geometric shapes consisting of lines (vertical, horizontal, diagonal, and right angled) and dots or squares (dots for 1st Armored and squares for 13th Armored), with HQ vehicles using triangles.

Chapter Three

Wargaming the Campaign

This chapter discusses the most important aspects of refighting the Desert War in miniature. Regardless of the rules you are going to use, the models you collect, or the size of battle you're going to recreate (whether brigade-scale or a tiny skirmish), certain campaign-specific wargaming ideas will really help to bring a feel for the Desert War to your tabletop. I discuss these important themes and ideas so that you can apply them to your own chosen rules; these are not a set of rules in their own right.

Combined Arms

Perhaps the most important aspect of the Desert War – and one that most wargame rules reflect in the miniature forces they suggest collecting – is the differing and evolving approaches to combined-arms operations adopted by both sides.

From their initiation to the Desert War, and based on their earlier experiences in Poland and France (and even the Spanish Civil War), the Germans fought using combined-arms tactics that threw together tanks, anti-tank guns, air support, and motorized infantry. Donald Featherstone summed up the use of combined arms by the Afrika Korps thus:

> German control of armour was superb … In action, tanks, anti-tank guns, recovery vehicles and petrol wagons, all supported by Stukas, went forward rapidly and successfully, often accompanied by senior officers. The co-operation between armour and the anti-tank gunners was exceptional, in fact the brilliant successes of the Afrika Korps depended upon three factors – the superior quality of their anti-tank

guns, the systematic practice of the principle of the co-operation of all arms, and their tactical methods …

The favourite German attack formation was in a block five or six abreast in line astern, with the heaviest armour in the van, anti-tank guns on the flanks with a sprinkling of motorized infantry. The main force of the motorized infantry were in the rear, covered by field artillery. In close support were the Stukas to deal with any obstinate British strongpoints. If repulsed, they would skilfully draw the British tanks onto their anti-tank guns – Rommel liked to get British armour to attack him when he would dispose his own armour behind carefully camouflaged anti-tank guns on which the British tanks were lured.

(Donald Featherstone, *Tank Battles in* Miniature, 1973, p. 39)

The German practice of retiring panzers back behind the safety of anti-tank guns was known as 'sword and shield' tactics and, as explained later, the British had little comeback against deployed ATGs until the arrival of the Lee/Grant tank.

The British used 'infantry-heavy' or 'tank-heavy' formations through the greater part of the campaign (until 1942), and suffered badly against their better organized German enemy. Early successes against disorganized Italian forces reinforced the British idea of tank- or infantry-heavy formations, which didn't help British military thinking a jot. Infantry-heavy forces were overrun by Afrika Korps panzers, and tank-heavy forces were blown apart by anti-tank guns.

Over time, the British followed suit and reorganized their forces in a similar way to the Germans. By 1942, the Allies were developing their own combined-arms tactics with British armoured formations dramatically overhauled in their organization during the Western Desert campaign. The British also excelled at combining artillery with other arms, especially from 1942 when General Auchinleck realized that concentrated divisional artillery support could smash the enemy advance to pieces. But even as early as Operation Battleaxe, German intelligence recorded that:

Reports stress the good cooperation between British tanks with their 85mm and 105mm artillery, which is very mobile as escorting artillery. The artillery fire is very accurately placed and is often directed by employing three armoured cars.

(quoted in T L Jentz, *Tank Combat in North Africa: The Opening Rounds*, 1998, p. 188)

Infantry assaults by all armies were often preceded by heavy artillery barrages; British terminology described two types of artillery support:

- The 'stonk': Hitting a large target area to distribute damage over many targets.
- The 'murder': Precision firing to remove a specific target.

American fire support was also good, both in terms of the number of barrels available and the fire-control equipment used to ensure accurate shooting.

When the Americans entered the Tunisian campaign, they faced a steep learning curve, pitting green units and commanders against the veteran (if by now ill-equipped and under-resourced) German and Italian defenders. Only through this baptism of fire did the Americans seem to take on board the lessons learned about combined arms tactics by the combatants of the Western Desert actions of 1941–42. But the Americans were quick learners, battle by battle, and by the invasion of Italy had moved on from the initial, scathing German assessment of American tactics: 'inflexible, plodding and all about material superiority'. Their material superiority remained, of course, throughout the remainder of the war. The Americans and British in Tunisia were well equipped with half-tracks for their infantry, and overwhelming artillery and aerial support, so found it easier to launch combined-arms assaults than had been the case for the combatants in the Western Desert.

Earlier, through 1940 and 1941, ad hoc British 'Jock Columns' (named after their instigator, Lieutenant Colonel 'Jock' Campbell VC) sought to combine lorried infantry, armoured cards, portee (truck-mounted) ATGs, and towed 25pdrs as mobile, aggressive battlegroups. In part this was due to the lack of available tank support, but also as a reaction to the (unsuccessful) British strategy of using tanks as the main strike force, relegating other units to support and consolidation duties.

An important element of most combined-arms forces is the ability for the infantry to keep pace with AFVs; without motorized infantry, a combined arms force on the tabletop will become as fragmented and ineffective as its real life counterpart, with huge gaps appearing between the fast-moving tanks and 3mph walking speed of foot troops. The North African campaign was characterized by motorized infantry more than any other theatre of the Second World War; virtually all German infantry forces were capable of travelling in trucks or the ubiquitous Sdkfz 251 'Hanomag' half-track; the British used the fully-tracked Bren Carrier and trucks; the Americans the M3 half-track and trucks; early in the campaign Italian infantry suffered from a lack of transport, but later were equipped with trucks. On the wargames table, there are several distinct ways to represent motorized infantry, each of which is valid depending on the level of game you're playing:

- Represent infantry units on foot and provide separate transport units that move and fight independently but may carry infantry in them. The infantry are destroyed if they're in their transport when it is destroyed, and are less vulnerable when on foot. This often leads to transports dropping troops off in the first couple of turns of a game and then retreating off the table. Half-tracks armed with machineguns may choose to stick around to provide some additional fire support. This works well for games at Company level or lower.
- Represent infantry units on foot, but if they are motorized or mechanized infantry, allow them to make a longer distance move in the first turn of the game (to represent their arrival in trucks without the need to model any trucks in your collection).
- Represent infantry units on foot with integrated transport models – either half tracks or trucks. The unit fights as dismounted infantry, but moves as though in vehicles. This simplifies things considerably but allows infantry to keep pace with other units. Given the level of abstraction used, this works better for Battalion and higher level games.

The same consideration should be given to towed artillery – do you need to represent their limbers on the table, or are you happy just to model the guns and assume that limbers are available when required?

Most rules include army lists or guidelines for collecting a balanced force of infantry, AFVs, artillery, and associated support. These usually include combined-arms forces, as few players choose to field infantry- or tank-only forces for the very same reasons the British discovered in 1941! It's generally a case of reverse engineering if you *do not* wish to field a combined-arms force – strip out the motorized infantry support from your armoured squadron, or remove the platoon of tanks allowed to your infantry company. Depending on your opponent's chosen force and the scenario being played, you may find your own units to be greatly inadequate for the task in hand, or mismatched against their enemies, but at the very least, you'll be able to explore the challenges faced by non-combined-arms forces in the earlier stages of the campaign.

Terrain & Climate

At its most basic, a desert battle – especially one set in the Western Desert Campaign – is one of the quickest wargames you could wish to set up. Donald Featherstone, speaking specifically about wargaming the campaign, wrote that:

> To reproduce this stark and semi-featureless expanse within the confines of a room or on a table-top may sound a difficult proposition. But in practice it is perhaps one of the easiest of all wargaming terrains to set up and can be made to look extremely realistic with a minimum effort. Perhaps this is because the Western Desert, and indeed all deserts … Bear the hallmark of space.
>
> (Donald Featherstone, *Tank Battles in Miniature*, 1973, p. 46)

A sandy-coloured sheet or terrain mat, with a scattering of low hills serves many Desert War players adequately, although it's easy enough to add other terrain features or model the terrain in detail on purpose-built boards. Terrain typically found on Desert War tables includes:

- **Hills or sand dunes:** these will block line of sight, offer tanks the cover to go hull-down behind, and may be difficult for heavier vehicles to cross.
- **Inhabited areas:** These should be few and far between, but villages and railway stops provide suitable 'stop points' to hold back an advancing enemy at. These provide good cover, block line of sight, and also enhance visibility from within as the defenders can take to the flat roofs for added elevation.
- **Oasis:** You can't have a desert wargame without an oasis on the tabletop – it's the law! But seriously, they shouldn't be uncommon on your table but restrict yourself to only one… this is an arid landscape after all. The water may be impassable, and the lush vegetation should provide soft cover for troops within.
- **Roads and tracks:** If encountered at all, they are unlikely to be well maintained; their only practical use on the tabletop is to pick an easier path through other, rougher terrain.
- **Rocky ground:** broken terrain of this type will provide cover for infantry, be impassable to wheeled vehicles, and some of the less mechanically reliable tanks may need to test for track shedding if they traverse this area.
- **Scrub:** Scrub provides soft cover for infantry, and may also slow their movement. It has no effect for vehicles.
- **Soft sand:** May cause vehicles to test for bogging down when crossing.
- **Wadis:** Wadis should be common terrain features. In the rainy season (autumn), a wadi will be a fast flowing stream or river – due to the rocky sides it will likely be impassable. At other times of the year it provides a natural trench, ideal for infantry to take cover in, and possibly vehicles too (depending on the size of the wadi); even when dry, a wadi will be difficult – or impossible – for vehicles to cross away from recognized pathways. The rocky surface may slow movement.

Tunisia's geography and geology is a little more varied: although some areas were similar to the Western Desert, much of the terrain fought over was dominated by hills and rocky ground, and in some areas, vegetation is far more common and even quite green. Scrub should be common, and there is a stronger possibility of inhabited areas on the tabletop than in the Western Desert. In general, Tunisia-themed tabletops should favour infantry and be harder work for vehicles to cross.

Wargamers rarely worry about climate's effect on their gaming beyond whether to open a window or not, but to ignore this factor in the Desert War means that you'll be missing out on some of the fun of gaming this period. Paddy Griffith noted of the North African terrain:

> Its very openness made it notoriously difficult for anyone to find cover, so that entire divisions might sometimes have to form up facing each other in the open, within artillery range, in a way that had not been seen since the middle of the 19th century... It was also extremely difficult to navigate accurately, and many are the stories of vehicles being lost for hours on end... In the summer the mirages could cause multiple distortions of the light that made observation, and range-finding by optical instruments, impossible. The rockier patches might resist the excavation of foxholes ... while the heat, the flies and the sandstorms constantly mocked all the normal expectations of 'civilized' warfare.
>
> (Paddy Griffith, *World War II Desert Tactics*, 2008, p. 4)

This excerpt alone lists many factors that may be introduced to your battles to add 'fog of war' or uncertainty to your battlefield; discussing terrain effects before the game begins makes perfect sense in Desert War wargames, and the variable effects of climate can make the same scenario play out very differently time and again.

Heat hazes might affect line of sight or even create mirages – if you play a game using an umpire, he or she may represent this by placing terrain features then removing them or changing them as your units get closer. This is not a twist to employ often, but can be fun once in a while.

More common were sand storms and dust clouds. The former reduced visibility – sometimes to zero – and increased the chance of units becoming lost or breaking down. Fighting a tabletop battle through a sandstorm would massively decrease ranges and movement distances, and so is perhaps best left to the most adventurous of players (or those refighting Sidi Barrani, where a sandstorm played a significant role in covering the attack). Instead, you could either test before the game begins to see whether the entire battle is fought under sand storm conditions (perhaps on the roll of a 6 on one six-sided die after deployment but before the first turn starts), or make the same test at the start of every turn of a game to see if the storms starts (and then stops when the next 6 is rolled).

Dust clouds, however, are great fun to use on the tabletop! As a unit moves across the sandy Western Desert, especially one in fast tanks or large numbers of trucks, it throws up a huge cloud of dust behind it. This will be visible from distance, even though the unit causing the cloud cannot be seen. This means that, as a commander, you know *something* is there, but not *what* it is, or *whom* it belongs to. On the wargames table, this can be used in one of two ways:

- At deployment, players do not place units, but instead deploy dust cloud markers. Some represent actual units, others are 'bluffs' or 'blinds' representing no significant military presence. Move all of them at a set pace (usually that of infantry) until one of your markers is close enough to attempt to spot or has line of sight of any enemy marker. At this point, both players reveal the cause of their dust cloud!
- In a scenario using reinforcements, allow players to introduce dust cloud markers as above, and reveal them in the same way. Allow one marker for each reinforcement unit available, and a handful of 'blinds'. Markers for actual units may only be introduced when allowed by the scenario rules, but 'blinds' may be brought into play as and when the owner chooses. Don't allow too many 'blinds' in this instance, otherwise players will become very blasé about their appearance.

The hostile desert environment exacerbated the problem of mechanical reliability for vehicles, notably for British and Italian AFV designs. Narrow tracks bogged down in soft sand or broke on rocky ground, and breakdowns were common over long distances. Sand caused all sorts of mechanical problems, not only to vehicle crews but to all who served. However, the added difficulty faced by the British and Italian tankers is worth reflecting on the tabletop: perhaps a mechanism even as harsh as rolling a six-sided die for every British or Italian tank unit (of those types listed as unreliable in Chapter Two) at the start of the game. On a roll of 1, the unit must lose a tank to mechanical failure before it reaches the battlefield (therefore not counting as a loss for victory purposes, but certainly as paid-for-but-lost army building points in the game).

Line of sight

The desert is not a billiard table-smooth surface, although in the pursuit of playability (and convenience), many tabletops take on just such an appearance. Perfectly good games may be played out across such boards, where the absence of cover means than gunnery range and line of sight (or spotting) become important aspects of game play. The terrain previously discussed naturally has an effect on line of sight, but even across open ground, the heat and glare of the desert affected visibility more than may at first be imagined.

Alongside the German tanks' ability to outrange their Allied adversaries, they were also at an advantage when spotting the enemy, as their panzers and artillery had superior optical equipment. This helped the Germans to lay down accurate fire at longer ranges than their opponents.

Due to the relatively open nature of desert warfare, smoke was a useful tool; it could be laid down from tanks (the British even used specialist 'Close Support' tanks that fired only smoke), infantry mortars (both the platoon light mortar and heavier tubes), and by artillery batteries. Smoke could be used both to conceal movement and to mark objectives for further attention.

The ever-reliable and inspiring Donald Featherstone produced a chart for visibility of enemy vehicles in the desert (1973), presenting visibility ranges at varying times of the day:

	Vehicle not moving	Single vehicle dust-cloud	Mass vehicles dust-cloud
Dawn	500 yards	750 yards	1,000 yards
Morning to noon	2,000 yards	3,000 yards	4,000 yards
12pm to 2pm	1,000 yards	1,500 yards	2,000 yards
2pm to 6pm	2,000 yards	3,000 yards	4,000 yards
Evening	500 yards	750 yards	1,000 yards
Evening, looking into the sun	250 yards	500 yards	750 yards

Tank Tactics

Many wargamers are drawn to the North African theatre by the lure of tanks. Bruce Quarrie wrote of the North African campaign:

> The vast open spaces of the North African desert form an almost ideal battleground for mechanized forces, comprising wide open areas for tactical manoeuvre with no crowded urban areas to interfere with the serious business of fighting. Being largely flat, they are also excellent for fast-moving armoured battles, although sand, dust and heat take their toll of both men and machines.
>
> (Bruce Quarrie, *Armoured Wargaming*, 1988, pp. 95–6)

This is a view that many wargamers subscribe to, and a suitably satisfying environment it is for armoured wargaming. However, as a note of caution, Paddy Griffith (as discussed more fully in the section on terrain) warned that:

> It turned out that the vast, bare landscape fell very far short of a tactician's dream, and for a wide variety of reasons.
>
> (Paddy Griffith, *World War II Desert Tactics*, 2008, p. 4)

Despite this, for many people – me included – the Desert War is the ideal setting for large armoured battles. Most rules reflect a general superiority of German AFVs over their British-designed enemies (the plentiful drawbacks of British AFVs are discussed below). In truth, until the Germans up-gunned to long barrelled 50mm and 75mm guns, there was less difference between AFV armaments than is often imagined; however, British cruiser tanks were notoriously under-armoured, leaving only the Matilda as a viable fighting vehicle in toe-to-toe battling. British cruisers fared far better against their Italian equivalents, however, which were equally poorly armoured and mechanically unreliable, and unable to pack a punch any better than the British anti-tank guns could. The introduction of the US-built M3 Medium Lee/Grant finally gave the British (and, later, the Americans) a tank that could fight against Panzer IIIs on an even footing, and the arrival of the M4 Sherman gave the Allies a better chance against the Panzer IV. The British Churchill and Valentine replaced the rapidly declining Matilda, and their chief strength – aside from good armour – was the capacity of both tanks' turrets to have 6pdr or 75mm guns squeezed in.

The German Panzer III and IV were both well-designed, reliable AFVs capable of being up-armoured and up-gunned, but the advantages presented by superior workmanship were often outweighed (or at least anchored down) by the limited number of AFVs the Germans were able to field at any given time in the campaign.

Aside from tank numbers in the field and their strengths and weaknesses in guns and armour, the upper hand was usually held by the side using the best tactics. And in general in the Desert War, this was the Germans. The section on Combined Arms explores the greatest reason for German ascendancy, although the battlefield experience of German troops in Africa was generally higher than that of their opponents, especially against the fresh British and American units they fought in Tunisia.

German tank tactics were based on a two-wave assault, striking with the first wave while fresh tank companies were brought up from the second wave to press the attack, exploit weaknesses, and replace first-wave casualties. German tactical directives required, amongst other things:

- To tackle enemy tanks as soon as they appear – abandon the current task to do so.
- Destroy enemy forces by concentration of strength.
- Pull back from enemy surprise attacks, gaining time to establish a better fire front. Mask the movement of the rear wave of tanks and use smoke to disguise movements.
- Move and fire: movement takes the enemy by surprise and allows superior firepower to be gathered for a decisive strike.
- The side which builds superior firepower and hits first will win.
- Smoke screens provide protection against aimed fire and time to establish a fire front.
- Fire is most effective from stationary panzers. (German assessments of British tank tactics noted that British fire was generally inaccurate as it was conducted on the move.)
- Attacks against enemy flanks and rear are most effective – use combat reconnaissance to achieve this.
- Combine attacks with anti-tank and infantry units. Infantry support by observation and reconnaissance, and with heavy weapons; anti-tank guns secure flanks and may be deployed to the rear using German tanks as 'bait'; artillery pins down enemy anti-tank guns and infantry, and concentrates fire against enemy tanks where terrain features constrict enemy tank movement.

German tank manuals of 1940 and 1941 summed up the decisive factors of tank versus tank combat as follows:

- Knowledge of automotive and weapons capabilities.
- Timely recognition and identification of the strength and direction of the enemy tank attack.
- A lightning-fast grasp of the situation and terrain as well as immediate action at all command levels.

(quoted in T L Jentz, *Tank Combat In North Africa*, 1998, p. 78)

These directives could easily have been written as 'advice for wargamers'; heed them well on the tabletop.

British tanks often fought in formations known as 'One Up' or 'Two Up': one (or two) squadrons in advance and the remaining squadrons in support. The idea behind this was to drive a wedge into the enemy's position ('One Up'), or to fight an enemy deployed over a wider front than one squadron could manage ('Two Up'); therefore, there was always a squadron in reserve. The 'One Up' formation was reminiscent of a cavalry charge, flying forward in the face of enemy guns, and often with a disastrous outcome given the cruiser tanks' lack of armour. Paddy Griffith described the British Royal Tank Regiment's thinking – or lack of it:

> When it arrived in the desert the RTR was keen to use not only mobility but also its ultimate expression in the head-down charge, or what came to be known – ominously – as 'Balaklavaring'.
>
> (Paddy Griffith, *World War II Desert Tactics*, 2008, p. 15)

Donald Featherstone described British armoured tactics as follows, noting how they evolved with experience:

> The standard British tank tactical formation was the arrowhead which allowed each tank to give good fire support to its neighbours, providing at the same time a fairly good defensive formation against anti-tank gunfire. Being under-gunned and under-armoured, the British were forced to resort to tactics of ambush or rushing in as quickly and as close as possible, accepting losses in the hope of dealing a quick knock-out blow.
>
> (Donald Featherstone, *Tank Battles in Miniature*, 1973, p. 41)

The British learned that the Panzers liked to back off, showing as little movement as possible and protecting their side armour. The British, with their less protected armour, got under cover and waited for the enemy to appear then they fired one quick shot and were away to the next mound, leapfrogging with another tank to keep some sort of cover.

> (Donald Featherstone, *Tank Battles in Miniature*, 1973, p. 40)

British tactical doctrine initially preached firing on the move, although experience came to show that fire-and-move was more useful and certainly more accurate. Smoke was considered an important concealment – early in the campaign, each Squadron was equipped with two tanks only capable of firing smoke (which was not available to the standard British tank gun at that time); the lack of widespread HE firepower proved problematic against dug-in anti-tank guns and soft targets. Gaining vital tank battle experience, the British eventually ditched the headlong charge (most of the time!), using fire and move tactics to advance using available cover – finally on a par with their German counterparts.

British armoured tactics were not aided by the interwar tank doctrine practiced in the UK: rather than focusing on a 'universal' tank (of which both the Panzer III and IV are good examples), the British developed tanks with specific roles in mind. By the start of the Second World War, British armoured units were equipped with tanks fulfilling one of three roles:

- **Infantry tanks:** Heavily armoured tanks designed to support infantry assaults; slow-moving and armed with machine-guns and anti-tank gun. Including the Matilda II and, later, Valentine.
- **Light tanks:** Small and lightly armoured, these were designed for reconnaissance tasks. Speed was their main advantage, and they fared badly when required to act as battle tanks. By the Desert War, the only remaining light tanks were Vickers Mk VI, although later in the campaign the Stuart/Honey may be considered in this category.
- **Cruiser tanks:** Cruisers were intended to balance speed and firepower, exploiting breakthroughs and manoeuvring behind enemy lines to break down communications and supply lines 'like cavalry'. Armed with machine-guns and anti-tank gun. Including the A9, A10 (technically a 'heavy cruiser' falling between the Cruiser and Infantry tank roles), A13, and Crusader.

Until the introduction of the 6pdr (57mm) in 1942, British tanks were armed only with a 2pdr (40mm) anti-tank gun. This was a formidable weapon at the outbreak of war (it could penetrate a whopping 57.5mm of armour at 500 yards), but by 1941 it was out-ranged by German 75mm and 88mm guns, and outfoxed by the increasing thickness of German armour. Although capable of firing HE shells, the small size of explosion was deemed ineffective so British tanks armed with the 2pdr could use only machine-guns against soft targets (the same was true of the later 6pdr gun). This proved a real shortcoming in the desert, where infantry anti-tank guns were able to target British tanks from beyond machine-gun range, meaning that the tank crews had no effective response. Most wargame rules do manage to reflect this problem, preventing 2pdr and 6pdr-armed British tanks from firing HE shots. The American-built Stuart fared no better with its 37mm gun, but the introduction of the Lee/Grant and then Sherman finally gave British armour a competitive HE gun.

Italian armour was mostly ineffective; early in the campaign, it was continually bested by British armour (in a technical sense, the British tanks were not much better than those of the Italians but, crucially, were equipped with better radio equipment). With the arrival of the Afrika Korps, Italian tanks seem to have employed German tactics, albeit using inferior equipment.

American tank units were tactically ill-equipped in Tunisia, having been rushed to the theatre without any tank-versus-tank tactical training. But battle tanks were not the only anti-tank AFVs equipping American armoured formations – in fact, the general theory was that tanks such as the Sherman would provide infantry support and separate 'tank destroyer' battalions would tackle enemy armour. Rather than being equipped with 'tanks', tank destroyer units fielded three types of vehicle:

- Unarmoured M6 trucks mounting a 37mm ATG.
- Lightly armoured, open topped M3 halftracks mounting 75mm field guns.
- M10 self-propelled guns based on the Sherman chassis, mounting a 3" ATG in an open turret.

In theory, these tank destroyer units would be placed in ambush positions using terrain to their advantage; as it happened, the battlefields of Tunisia were fairly well suited to this tactic, although the thin armour of the trucks and halftracks meant that they couldn't stand against enemy armour in a firefight, instead needing to use their speed of movement and low profile to find an advantageous position in cover.

Cover was used by all tank units where available. In both the Western Desert and Tunisia, 'hull down' was the most common concealment a tank could achieve; Donald Featherstone described this position well:

> A tank is 'hull-down' when it is so positioned that its hull is hidden and only its turret (and gun) can be seen. In this way, the vehicle can come into action whilst achieving the maximum possible protection. In the barren and cruel drabness of the Desert, the undulations that afforded hull-down cover were often only shoulders of grey grit but, in such circumstances, they represented important high ground.
> (Donald Featherstone, *Tank Battles in Miniature*, 1973, p. 40)

On the tabletop, hull-down should count as good cover. However, it can be difficult to establish what actually counts as hull-down, as most tables lack the subtle contours of a 1:1 battlefield, and model hills come in one of two types: flat topped with sharp sloped edges, and gradual slopes building to a crest. Neither works very well for placing a tank in a hull down position. Unless guidelines for this important tank tactic are included in your rules of choice, I recommend trying the following ideas; either:

- Allow any tank that is in contact with the top of a hill to count as hull down when viewed from the opposite side – even if the model itself sits on the crest of the hill.
- Take a more abstract approach, and allow any tank to become 'hull down' if it spends a turn stationary during its movement phase. You may wish to designate some areas of the board unsuitable for this to take place, to prevent all tanks finding cover too easily.

Norman Plough, commanding a troop of A13 cruiser tanks in A Squadron, 2nd Royal Tank Regiment (2 RTR), fought at Beda Fomm and recalled the small unit tactics used there:

We were hull-down below the low ridge. Two groups of M-13 tanks from the 1st Ariete Armoured Division, recently arrived at Benghazi, attacked our position. The first group in two waves was destroyed without loss to us.

The second group about 40 minutes later advanced down our right flank and three of our A-13s moved across to the Arab grave cairns and tombs. About the same time a few M-13s advanced down the east side of the road and knocked out Lieutenant Henry Dumas's tank. I joined him for a few minutes while he took over one of the other troop tanks. This second group of M-13s was also destroyed or withdrew from the action. The Italian tank crews were 'green' with little battlefield experience. Their tactics were poor. We were lucky. We had protection from the mound and road defile, they had none and had to advance across open ground.

(Quoted in Patrick Delaforce, *Battles With Panzers*, 2003, p. 184)

Applying realistic tank tactics to your own game is very much a matter of personal choice. Few rules reward the British 'Balaklavering' across the table, or prevent the Germans from doing the same (although *Flames of War* does include rules allowing the British certain bonuses for such actions in their cruiser tanks). Jumping from cover to cover works well unless your opponent is allowed to use opportunity (or reaction) fire. Using the German tactic of retiring AFVs to lead the enemy into an ATG ambush position is hard to achieve unless your rules of choice allow for hidden deployment – and if they don't, this is something you could consider introducing specifically for ATGs and dug-in infantry (don't place them on the table at the start of the game, but note down their exact position and reveal them when you wish to fire, or if the enemy gets within spotting distance).

Conversely, the differences in tank guns and armour thickness are usually handled very well by rules. Some 'crunchy' rule sets apply a huge number of ratings for armour (including differences in side and rear armour), and break down the armour penetration of ATGs by range. Others follow a simpler route, rating different tank types as having 'light', 'medium', or 'heavy' armour, and applying the same ratings for ATGs. Both are equally valid – it's a matter of personal taste, and to some extent, the level of game you're playing (a 1mm difference in armour thickness should make little difference between tank units in a Battalion level wargame).

Tank and anti-tank guns

The anti-tank gun table shown in Chapter 2 gives some indication of the relative performances of the different ATGs used in the Desert War. More than any other aspect of armoured warfare, anti-tank guns saw the greatest strides forward across the course of the campaign – armour penetration and range were vital battle winners in the Western Desert especially, and both sides accordingly up-gunned their AFV designs wherever possible.

Allied crews – especially those battling with the British 2pdr – had an inferiority complex about their anti-tank weapons. With regard to the performance of the maligned British 2pdr against enemy guns, Donald Featherstone voiced the opinion that:

> the German high velocity 50mm anti-tank gun was far superior to the British 2pdr and batches of these guns always accompanied German armour into action. On the other hand the British restricted their 3.7 inch anti-aircraft guns [slightly larger in calibre to the German 88mm Flak and of potentially similar AT performance] to an anti-aircraft role and regarded the anti-tank gun as a defensive weapon.
>
> (Donald Featherstone, *Tank Battles in Miniature*, 1973, p. 40)

And:

> The 88mm gun could out-range the 2pdr by more than 2,000 yards and was frequently known to knock out a tank at 3,000 yards. This meant that the British tanks had to tensely run the gauntlet of this fire until they were within the effective range of their own 2pdr pea-shooters.
>
> (Donald Featherstone, *Tank Battles in Miniature*, 1973, p. 94)

Bob Crisp of 3 RTR felt that the odds were stacked against the British, describing British tank crew morale at the Battle of Sidi Rezegh in 1941:

> Sneaking through the battalion on our side were disturbing stories that the Honeys and Crusaders were no match at all for the Mark IIIs and Mark IVs in equal combat. It was a simple proposition: our little cannons could not knock them out, and they could knock us out easily. Within the week we were reckoning that it needed three Honeys to destroy one Mark IV.
> (Quoted in Patrick Delaforce, *Taming the Panzers*, 2000, p. 70)

Aside from issues of armour penetration, the type of shell fired by AFVs against unlimbered anti-tank guns also had a critical impact on battle. ATGs were generally low-profile weapons, hard to hit and even more so when dug in. The obvious way to remove their threat was to fire HE shells to kill or drive away the crew and possibly put the gun out of commission. For most tanks, the only issue here was being able to spot such small targets, and then to strike first (harder than it might seem, as the stability of unlimbered ATGs usually gave them an advantage in accurate fire over range). For British 2pdr (and the 6pdr with its limited HE capability), this was not possible – the AFV would need to register a direct hit on the ATG's frame, or move close enough to use machineguns. No easy thing!

The situation for the British (and Americans) improved with the introduction of the Lee/Grant and, later, Sherman tanks. These US-built tanks had reasonable armour piercing and good HE performance. The iconic Lee and Grant tanks (which were almost identical – the Grant was modified for British requirements) made their debut at Gazala, and the crews generally felt that this brought them onto a par with their Afrika Korps counterparts. It was not, however, perfect. Jim Caswell of 3 RTR wrote of the Grant tanks issued to his squadron:

> They had a 37mm and machine-guns in the turret and a 75mm gun at the side of the tank – a match for German guns, but because it was not in the turret, it only had a 25 per cent traverse… The new tanks were also quite high and squat … thereby presenting a better target

for the enemy... Some engines were diesel, some petrol. There was always a fight for the diesels because they did not catch fire as easily as the petrol ones did.

(Quoted in Patrick Delaforce,
Taming the Panzers, 2000, pp. 83–4)

At the very end of the Desert War, in Tunisia, the British debuted the 17pdr ATG (at this stage, mounted on a 25pdr gun carriage and named the Pheasant), which had an anti-tank capability similar to the German 88mm.

In game terms, some of the crucial factors to consider when it comes to anti-tank gunnery include:

- **Damage caused by penetration**
  - Splintering: Fragments of the shell or tank parts ricocheting inside the hull or turret, causing death or injury to the crew.
  - Fatal equipment damage: A shot passing through an AFV's armour would mean that any vital piece of equipment within the tank may suffer irreparable damage, either causing the tank to become non-functioning or reduce efficiency.
  - Explosion: Caused either by HE shell or by a vital part of the targeted tank igniting (ammo, fuel, etc), with little chance of the crew surviving. Sherman and Matilda II tanks were notorious for catching on fire easily; some AFVs used 'wet stowage' to minimize the chances of ammo detonating.
- **Damage caused by non-penetration**
  - Mobility: A non-penetrating hit could temporarily or permanently damage the AFV's running gear – and an immobile tank is a sitting duck.
  - Gun damage: There was a small chance of a direct hit on an AFV's main gun – if this happened, the tank would be of little use until repaired.
  - Psychological effect: Hits from smaller calibre weapons (which was consistently recalled by tank crews as sounding like heavy rain), non-penetrating hits, or shells passing straight through a tank's armour and

out the other side would all have an effect on the crew, who may bail out, lose focus trying to identify where the shots came from, panic, and so on.

- **Crew bail out:** Either from penetrating or non-penetrating shots, the crew might decide they've had enough and temporarily or permanently abandon the tank. In gaming terms, this also often represents the crew being shocked or stunned inside the vehicle, rather than jumping out through a hatch.

Depending on the level of game you're playing, you may wish to introduce a 'damage chart' featuring the above outcomes, rather than the all-or-nothing approach of 'tank destroyed' or 'missed shot'. As a general rule, the higher the calibre of the shell, the higher the chance of significant damage after penetration (incidentally, this is something that the popular *Flames of War* rules model rather well – see Chapter Four).

Donald Featherstone (1973) produced a very enlightening table to demonstrate the hit probabilities of Second World War tank guns:

	500 yards	1,000 yards	1,500 yards	2,000 yards	2,500 yards
9 foot high target	78%	37%	10%	2%	1%
3 foot high target	45%	21%	6%	1%	–
2nd shot on target	95%	90%	80%	20%	15%

Turning these into a direct translation on the tabletop, using percentage dice (roll one 10-sided die for the 'tens', and another for the 'ones'... a 7 and a 3 equalling 73 per cent), would make for a very different style of armour battle, depending on the ground scale you use!

8mm Perry Miniatures British infantry supported by a Blitzkrieg-manufactured Matilda II tank. (*Michael Perry, Perry Miniatures*)

Perry Miniatures Pak38 (50mm calibre) anti-tank gun. (*Michael Perry, Perry Miniatures*)

Rommel at large (or at least in 28mm)! (*Michael Perry, Perry Miniatures*)

28mm Perry Miniatures Afrika Korps, demonstrating the wide variety of uniform shades found in the desert. (*Michael Perry, Perry Miniatures*)

28mm Perry Miniatures British infantry supported by a Marmon-Herrington armoured car and Vickers VI light tank. (*Michael Perry, Perry Miniatures*)

A close up of 28mm hard plastic Perry Miniatures Desert Rats, possibly headed by miniature versions of the Twins themselves! (*Michael Perry, Perry Miniatures*)

A 6mm GHQ British infantry platoon; note Lee Hadley's great idea for identifying what is on each tiny stand – a subtly printed ID at the rear of each. (*Lee Hadley*)

28mm British Crusader I tanks and a Bren Carrier. (*Michael Perry, Perry Miniatures*)

28mm Perry Miniatures German *Fallschirmjäger* paratroopers, who fought as ground-based elite infantry in North Africa. (*Michael Perry, Perry Miniatures*)

An old warhorse! 15mm British A10 cruiser tank by Plastic Soldier Company. (*Plastic Soldier Company*)

A familiar sight for gamers fielding a British cruiser force: 'breakdown'. From the early A9 and A10 tanks to this Crusader II, all marques were mechanically unreliable and some rules allow for this. (*Wargames Illustrated*)

28mm Artizan German troops and armoured car in Tunisia. (*Wargames Illustrated*)

28mm Artizan British or Commonwealth infantry in the Tunisia campaign, supported by a Vickers MG. (*Wargames Illustrated*)

15mm Battlefront British and German forces meet in 1941; note the Caunter camouflage scheme on the British A13 tanks. (*Wargames Illustrated*)

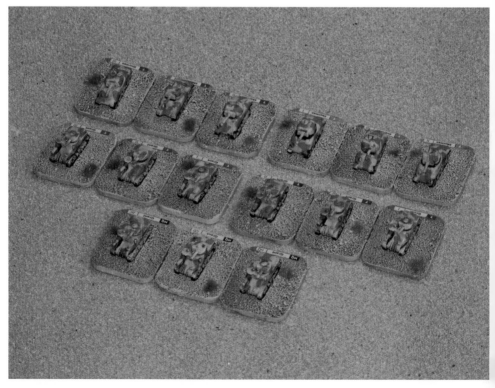

A British Heavy Armoured Squadron in 6mm; Grant tanks supported by Shermans. (*Lee Hadley*)

The famous – infamous – German 88mm ATG. 15mm Battlefront model. (*Neil Reinwald*)

Neil Reinwald's 15mm Afrika Korps force for Flames of War, suitable for both the Western Desert and Tunisian campaigns. (*Neil Reinwald*)

15mm Battlefront Panzer III tank. (*Neil Reinwald*)

Italian armour in 6mm; these tanks are the M14/41, a version of the M13/40 with an upgraded engine. (*Lee Hadley*)

Superbly painted 6mm German Tiger tanks – this trio of models would represent a significant proportion of the number of real Tigers deployed in Tunisia! (*Lee Hadley*)

Infantry Tactics

The key role of infantry in the battles of the North African campaign generally fell into one of the following categories:

- Assaulting enemy positions (usually on foot, although the Germans and Americans preferred bringing their infantry directly into battle in halftracks).
- Holding defensive positions (preferably dug-in, with good ATG positions, barbed wire, and minefields).

However, Donald Featherstone wrote dismissively of infantry in the desert, in a way that perhaps only a Royal Tank Regiment veteran of the campaign could:

> The main lesson learned in the Desert fighting was that infantry, unless much better equipped to deal with armour, were an embarrassment. Once their tanks had gone, the infantry had lost their hard armoured coating so that it was not possible to meet the enemy in the open desert. This meant that the infantry became a liability instead of an asset and were largely at the mercy of enemy tanks.

He does (slightly) relent by noting:

> Later in the campaign, the infantry showed what they could do when properly equipped but when they were not they could do nothing except fight gallantly against great odds.
> (Donald Featherstone, *Tank Battles in Miniature*, 1973, p. 38)

I think it is fair to say that Featherstone was almost certainly writing mostly with the larger-scale engagement in mind, although General Sir Claude Auchinleck reported a similar sentiment to Churchill. Infantry come into their own in smaller-scale engagements, and in terrain other than open desert... even somewhat in open desert if they are well fortified. And of course, if you want to hold that ground that your artillery has beaten flat or your tanks have cruised through the enemy to reach, who is going to be able to dig in and hold it against counter-attacks other than your infantry and their associated support weapons (heavy mortars, anti-tank guns, field guns, heavy machine-guns, and so on)?

Depending on the scale of game you wish to play, the way infantry are used in your games will vary. For the large-scale battles mentioned above, where units on the table represent platoons or companies as the smallest group, it's unusual for individual weapons to matter; however, if you're playing a skirmish game reflecting squad or platoon level tactics, it will make a difference where on the table your platoon mortar is, which model carries the LMG, and so forth. Basically, don't dismiss the option of playing an engrossing game set in the desert using infantry… refighting a tiny section of a major battle – or the outcome of two small patrols meeting – without much in the way of AFV support on the table. It can be a huge test of your tactical ability, especially when playing across a table with limited opportunity for taking cover.

In 1940 and 1941 the British favoured beginning infantry assaults under cover of darkness. In reality, delays and confusion at the starting lines frequently led to the assault being made as it became light, rather than achieving the element of surprise and confusion that was intended. If you are gaming an infantry assault, you may perhaps allow the attack to go ahead at night on a roll of 5 or 6 on a six-sided die (possibly just a 6 if you're so inclined) – which will limit lines of sight, and generally make things easier for the attackers, who should expect to be well equipped with reconnaissance intelligence of where and how the defences are organized.

A vivid description of small-scale infantry action is described by James Lucas.

The line halts. There's a whispered conference. There are about six Spandaus [German MGs] firing on our platoon front. Each of our sections will take out a couple. This is a game we've played before and we deploy, working forward, crouched and moving swiftly. As we get near our first Spandau, we are met with bursts from Schmeisser machine-pistols and the flat 'crack' of German hand grenades.

Crouching low, we swing higher up the slope moving from rock to rock. There are several very loud bangs – Mills bombs [British hand grenades] – away on our left. Then a few more ... The tracer stream coming from the Spandau dominating us suddenly flies into the dark sky and then stops. A bomb has obviously got the gunner. There is no more firing coming at us. The officer blows his whistle and we move uphill. It's been a cakewalk this time. All we have to do now is to dig and consolidate our hold on the position.

(James Lucas, *War in the Desert*, 1982, pp. 81–2)

The campaign in Tunisia was a different matter, as terrain was denser, hilly, and in places well fortified (along the Mareth Line), meaning that tanks and other AFVs needed infantry support. The terrain also meant that, at times, only infantry units could take the ground required. Parts of the Tunisian campaign may be fought in a manner more akin to the later battles in Italy – not least because infantry units were better equipped than ever before, frequently mechanized, and could rely on improved artillery support.

Platoons would generally advance in an arrowhead (one squad up, two in reserve) or 'V' formation (two squads up, one in reserve), using move-and-fire tactics at either half-squad or squad level. Companies took the same approach, with platoons advancing in arrowhead or 'V' formation.

At man-to-man levels, tactics varied by nation, mostly depending on the strengths offered by their weapons. For example:

- German squad and platoon tactics emphasized the importance of squad LMGs: the MG34's high rate of fire served as the squad's primary offensive weapon, with the riflemen carrying ammunition for it and deploying to defend the LMG's position and supplement it's firepower with their rifles.
- At the opposite extreme, American squads relied on their riflemen, armed with the semi-automatic M1 Garand – praised by General Patton as the 'greatest battle implement ever devised' – which could deliver a high rate of fire from the squad; the American LMG was the Browning Automatic Rifle, which was limited by a small magazine and low rate of

fire compared with the MG34 (see Chapter Two). Therefore, American squads relied on their rifles more than their LMG.

• Between the two extremes lay the British. Their Bren LMG was a good weapon – superior to the BAR but with a lower rate of fire than the MG34 – and was the focus of a squad's ('section' in British military parlance) firepower, supplemented by riflemen with a high percentage of skilled shots.

Stephen Bull's *World War II Infantry Tactics: Squad and Platoon* (Osprey, 2004) gives a good account of more specific national squad tactics in both defence and attack.

In game terms, German MGs often have a higher rate of fire or greater chance of hitting than those of their enemies, due to the excellent MG34 (and later MG42) used by their infantry. The American M1 Garand rifle was a semi-automatic weapon as opposed to being bolt operated, and many Squad or Platoon level rules allow American infantry to either fire and move (if not otherwise allowed within the rules) or an improved rate of fire over bolt-action rifles; rules designed for larger-scale battles usually ignore such tropes.

In addition to the squad weapons of rifle, SMG and LMG, infantry assaults relied upon support from light weapons held at platoon or company level, and heavier weapons deployed at battalion level or higher. Regardless of nationality, individual platoons could generate their own smoke and indirect fire with light mortars (2″ or 50mm tubes), and carried anti-tank rifles (or from 1942 onwards, more effective rocket-firing weapons such as bazookas and the British PIAT). Battalion and divisional support saw the deployment of larger-calibre mortars (with greater range and firepower), tripod-mounted MMGs, anti-tank and anti-aircraft gun assets, and tank support. Sometimes these were split out piecemeal between attacking infantry units, and at others were kept in their own platoons and deployed where most needed. Most wargame rules govern the use of support weapons, allowing a certain number dependent on how many rifle squads or companies you field. This prevents a player from fielding too unbalanced a force.

Alongside the infantry's own support platoons, assaults would often be preceded by longer-range artillery barrages; these can be incorporated into your games either by calling in strikes from on-table forward artillery observers (who can direct off-table artillery to shoot at whatever they can see from their position on-table), or for the attacking player to nominate a number of defending units to be targeted before the game begins, potentially softening them up before the on-table action gets going. In general, it's best to represent artillery off-table; some rules allow players to field artillery batteries on the tabletop – and let's face it, if you wish to collect artillery models, you'll want to use them in some way – but this brings with it an artificial role for weapons that rarely saw action as direct-fire weapons (exceptions do exist, of course, such as infantry support guns and heavier artillery used in an ATG role, such as the German 88mm and British 25pdr).

If you're refighting any the larger battles of the campaign or even playing a theoretical yet historically balanced encounter, infantry should comprise a substantial proportion of your force. The biggest challenge is how best to integrate them with the rest of your force: in general, rules allow AFVs and motorized transport to move swiftly across the tabletop, while the infantry crawl along at a snail's pace. Putting them in transport units usually makes them vulnerable to bombardment by artillery or air, and you'll end up fighting a game of two battles: one between the two armoured forces tearing around each other from the start of the game, and one of gradually moving your infantry support up, hoping they can arrive in time to achieve something. Scenarios with set objectives that must be held by infantry units somewhat balances this out (see Chapter Six). Another option is to begin with both infantry forces either dug in and playing a defensive role (not unlikely in real life), or deployed in an advanced position so they come into play sooner (the problem with this being the challenge of keeping them alive until the armoured 'cavalry' arrive).

In smaller level games – Company and below – this is less of a problem as both sides' main force will be infantry-based. In my view, this is the best way to fight a good infantry battle in the Desert War, leaving the sweeping manoeuvres of the larger battles to armoured units with support from stylized versions of motorized infantry (combining the armour and speed of their transport units with the staying power of dug-in infantry – something more common in board wargames than miniature wargames).

Platoon or Squad level skirmish games are all about the role of infantrymen. Once again, a good scenario helps here, along with a table laid out with more terrain than you might usually see on a desert-based tabletop. For this level of game, the smaller features seldom portrayed in wargames (such as small rocky outcrops, shallow dips in the ground level, and so on) become important areas of cover, so should be modelled. An infantry gamer's eyes are often turned west to consider the more cover-strewn battlefields of Tunisia for such games.

Supply Lines

Every successful breakthrough or pursuit in the seemingly limitless expanse of the desert made the quartermaster and logistics corps wince. A 10-mile advance required the supply lines from the rear echelon to stretch 10 miles further, adding time to bring materiel and men to the front, and using precious transport fuel to replenish precious combat fuel.

Elastic supply lines came with security risks too: desert raiders, enemy aircraft, and flanking manoeuvres close to the front line all endangered supply convoys and both sides knew to target them. Any success in the context of a wargame campaign should reflect the increasing difficulties faced the more successful a player is (which is a rare thing in gaming). Without supply, retreat must occur.

Aside from the basic needs of an army such as water, food, and fuel, keeping these increasingly mechanized forces in running condition threw up additional puzzles for the logistics corps.

The Germans mastered the concept of tank recovery well before their opponents. As a consequence, German AFVs with minor battle damage could be returned to the battle, having been located and towed away under cover of night; only later did the Allies operate a similarly efficient service. In a campaign game – or even in linked scenarios – you may choose to allow German forces a better chance of fielding damaged AFVs than their opponents. Recovery of a damaged vehicle makes the basis of a great skirmish scenario, too.

Standardization was not an oft-used word in the Desert War (although the Germans seem to have been better in this respect than the British and Italians) – it's not too big an exaggeration to say that the armies fought with what they could keep running, repair, or salvage as often as they waged war with the equipment their 'paper strength' indicated.

In game terms, this means that you can field understrength and/or mixed units, and even use captured enemy equipment (within reason). The Australians and British used captured Italian armour, and vice versa; more common at the start of the campaign, there's no reason that individual tanks cannot be 'repurposed' in later battles too. With regard to mixed-armour units, once again early in the campaign, it was not unusual for British armoured formations to mix the different cruisers and Vickers light tanks together in the same squadron (although rarely the same troop).

As an aside, if supply lines and the grand sweeping manoeuvres of the Desert War appeal to you, it's worth checking out the many excellent (if sometimes very complex) boardgames dedicated to refighting the campaign. The wonderfully named BoardGameGeek website is a great resource for this sort of wargame (online search: 'boardgamegeek').

Leadership and Morale

There are many ways to make characters of your leaders and commanders, either through roleplay or by introducing special rules to your games. The British suffered a succession of new commanders after every set-back, meaning that their troops suffered from a lack of consistent direction; depending on the commanders involved, sometimes this was for better, sometimes for worse!

Rommel – the Desert Fox – was renowned and feared in equal measure by his opponents; a great tactical mind – if not the complete strategist – his decisive leadership often put his forces on the front foot and at times he left the most conservative of British commanders reeling in confusion. A running joke among Desert War gamers is 'Rommel: +1'… whatever the reason for rolling your dice, if Rommel is leading your tabletop army, you may add one to the result to achieve a better outcome, such is his reputation amongst wargamers.

Aside from this slightly tongue in cheek '+1', various named leaders may grant morale bonuses, make their forces harder to rout by their very presence, or gain a tactical advantage during deployment or when fighting a certain style of combat (an inspired tank leader such as Pip Roberts VC, for example).

In addition to the qualities of your leaders, the quality of your units may have a significant impact on desert battles. Some units are fierce in close combat (Australians often get this bonus!), others have high morale (among Italian troops the Bersaglieri are mostly unique in this respect in wargame rules), and so on.

But the reputations of your metal or plastic units are not always positive.

Italian forces received a greater mauling from the Allied press and propaganda units than by perhaps any military units on the battlefield. Even now, they are remembered as poor soldiers who put up little fight, but this simply isn't true. Where Italian forces did suffer, however, was in poor or inexperienced leadership and unreliable equipment – which most likely led to poor morale as noted in Jon Latimer's *Operation Compass*:

> The Italians ... proved consistently that they did not lack individual courage. Innumerable examples are testament to their individual bravery. What they lacked was collective morale which, given the deficiencies of their military machine was hardly surprising, and was compounded by the vast gulf that existed between officers and men ...
>
> (John Latimer, *Operation Compass*, 2000, p. 93)

Often, the higher echelons of Italian command were uninspired, reliant upon out-dated tactics, or sometimes kept in the dark by their German allies. This notably 'un-special' relationship is exemplified by Italian units becoming surrounded and surrendering at Second El Alamein when their allies stole their transport to make a quick exit! Despite this, the Italian

Ariete performed well in support of the Afrika Korps, despite its poorer equipment. The Italian soldier in the field was not well led, and was hampered by poor-quality equipment (there was no standardization of rifle calibre, for example); if well dug-in and fighting on the defensive, however, it was frequently noted that Italian infantry could be hard to shift. This may be reflected in your morale rules – it can be fun to only roll for Italian morale and leadership once they meet the enemy, meaning that you never quite know which Italian force will turn up.

Aside from their far superior equipment, green American units entering Tunisia faced similar problems to the Italians with regard to inexperienced leaders – and although not lacking motivation, their troops were untested in combat and they faced various well-led Western Desert veterans. Erratic leadership and field performance led to a curious mixture of success and failure by the Americans in Tunisia, and American doctrine placed headquarters too far behind the front line to sustain a tight control over combat. If your rules allow, you may choose to make American units in Tunisia motivated and brave, but not especially well led (negative command modifiers twinned with positive morale modifiers throws up all sorts of challenges, somewhat offset by the superior numbers and kit fielded by US forces in Tunisia).

Morale among veterans on both sides was not always great: British armoured units gained a reputation for being 'sticky' and not endangering themselves unnecessarily. This can be difficult to model well on the tabletop; the *Flames of War* rules (see Chapter Four) do this well, by making some British units Reluctant Veterans – their morale goes down when they take casualties or become pinned, but they are difficult to hit in the first place. Once again, a mixture of positive and negative modifiers in other rule sets can recreate the psychological 'sticky' status: make these veterans harder to target, but easier to damage or pin when a hit makes contact.

Prepared Defences and Minefields

From the hand-dug slit trenches scraped out by infantrymen, to the German-held, French-built Mareth Line in Tunisia, prepared defences are an important factor when wargaming the Desert War.

The Mareth Line was a 25-mile system of concrete bunkers and prepared defences built in the 1930s by the French to defend their territory from Italian invasion. In the Tunisian campaign, it was defended by Axis forces against the British Eighth Army. In preparation for this, 62 miles of barbed wire, 100,000 anti-tank and 70,000 anti-personnel mines were laid along it. It was assaulted without success in March 1943, the British eventually executing a flanking manoeuvre remembered as the 'left hook' to bypass it and cut it off. On the tabletop, well-designed permanent concrete defences of this type should be very hard to break through and impervious to most gunfire other than direct hits and very large-calibre artillery barrages – luckily for the attacker, they were few and far between. Storming a bunker could make for an exciting skirmish game at squad or platoon level.

Defences around important strategic posts such as Tobruk – although not as formidable as the Mareth Line – were still hard to break through. Defended along the perimeter by minefields and copious amounts of barbed wire (and sometimes anti-tank ditches), low-profiled perimeter posts and larger forts were placed both along the line and further back to create defence in depth. These could range from pillboxes and sand-bagged strongpoints, to infantry-defended trench systems linking machine-gun and anti-tank positions. From a wargamer's perspective, these defences should offer good cover, but just as importantly, they were designed to slow down any assault, leaving the attacker in the open and vulnerable to counterattack and artillery barrage. Morale bonuses should be granted to the defenders of such defences – Italian units were reportedly much harder to overcome when defending a prepared perimeter and the prolonged sieges of Tobruk demonstrate that breaking in was no easy feat.

The frontier forts occupied by the Italians at the start of the Desert War proved less problematic. Their high walls proved a solid target for aerial bombing (Maddalena was hit by British Blenheim light bombers and capitulated shortly after), and tank guns and infantry weapons proved enough to persuade the garrison of Fort Capuzzo to surrender.

The British were keen on using a defensive 'box', for example at Gazala. This was an area held in brigade strength, primarily defended by anti-tank guns and artillery and, if possible, minefields. Strung out along a strategic perimeter, these boxes were not mutually supporting, so usually had to stand alone against inevitable enemy interest. Axis armour could assault the static defences, requiring Allied armour and other reinforcements to arrive in support, thus negating the original purpose of the box.

In addition to the more permanent defences noted above, infantry units at company level and below might build their own sangars – stone and sandbagged walls from which they could fire without exposing themselves to return fire. These would not stand up to heavy barrages, but in a small-scale tabletop action, such a position should be formidable to an attacking infantry force bereft of HE support.

Barbed wire has been mentioned above, and its tabletop effect should be to slow down movement through it. Infantry and tracked vehicles are especially slowed, but even tanks could become bogged down by the sheer number of wires snagged in their tracks and running gear. Explosive charges and wire-clearing equipment could be employed, but those tasked with such duties would inevitably become priority targets for the defenders. In a prepared defensive position, you may wish to rule that defenders can move through wire positions relatively quickly, as they should have been briefed on hard-to-spot safe paths through the bird's nest of wire.

'Achtung! Minen!' is a sign commonly modelled on the tabletop. Less frequently do games actually incorporate the minefields that dramatically shaped the movements of the opposing armies in North Africa. On the tabletop, minefields may either be clearly marked terrain features, or marked on a map in secret and only revealed when your enemy moves into it. There are four types of minefield that may be deployed:

- Anti-personnel: Affecting only infantry and possibly soft-skin vehicles.
- Anti-tank: Affecting vehicles only.
- Mixed: Combining both anti-tank and anti-personnel.
- Dummy: A marked area with no actual mines.

Unless your rules have specific minefield guidelines, use the following idea. When moving into a minefield, a unit should choose how it is going to move through:

- Snail's pace: Move at the slowest possible pace allowed by your rules (perhaps 1cm or 1"). At the end of the movement, roll a six-sided die. On a roll of 1 your unit takes a hit from the minefield.
- Cautiously: Move at up to half speed. At the end of the movement, roll a six-sided die. On a roll of 1 to 3 your unit takes a hit from the minefield.
- Go for broke: Move at full speed, with a 100 per cent chance of taking a hit from the minefield.

The strength of a hit from the minefield should be pretty powerful – perhaps the same as a medium or heavy-calibre field gun. Basically, if your unit is 'hit' by a mine, it should stand only a small chance of survival. And all the time a unit is moving slowly through a minefield, it is an easy target in open ground to the enemy.

Some rules allow you to field mine clearance tanks, or hand-held mine detectors. These are of course much safer to deploy when shells aren't flying over your head, but a stealthy night raid to clear a path through an enemy minefield would make for a tense squad level skirmish game.

Aerial Support

With regard to its effect on tabletop land battles, the role of aircraft in the Second World War is mostly limited to reconnaissance, close support and ground strafing. Aerial dogfights and heavy bombing raids are best played using specialist air combat wargame rules.

Although aircraft had been deployed in the initial clashes between British and Italian forces, the arrival of the Afrika Korps accelerated aerial support for ground-based operations. As had been demonstrated in Poland and France, German Blitzkrieg tactics saw co-operation between ground troops and the Luftwaffe, who provided ground support with Stuka dive bombers and other light bombers. The open spaces of the Desert War saw an increased role for ground-strafing fighters and fighter–bombers on both sides. Accordingly, ground troops were provided with anti-aircraft batteries to defend themselves. Air superiority came to play a part in the Desert War too – this could swing either way through much of the campaign, but after Operation Torch, the Allies will almost always possess superiority.

If you wish to include aerial support in your games – and I'd suggest that this in an intrinsic part of Battalion and higher-level wargames – there are several ways to do so. Some rules provide extensive guidelines for fielding aerial support, but if not, the following suggestions will be helpful:

- Use aircraft either for scheduled strikes on set turns of the game, or call them in using Forward Air Observers (or recon units) and then testing to see if the aircraft arrive (perhaps rolling two six-sided dice, successful on a 10+, or an 8+ if you have air superiority).
- Determine whether your aerial support is a dive bomber, light bomber, or ground-strafer. (Most likely, this will have been determined before the game begins).
- When your aircraft is due to arrive on the tabletop, allow the enemy to fire any anti-aircraft guns they have deployed on the table – unless your rules state otherwise, assume that their range covers the table for simplicity.
- If the aircraft survives, choose your target and make an attack. Dive bombers and ground-strafers make direct attacks (depending on their armament, this could be the equivalent of being hit by several machine-guns or an anti-tank gun); light bombers deliver the equivalent of an artillery barrage (most likely a light or medium battery, depending on the light bombers you have available).
- After making this attack, the aircraft is removed from play (but may return).

In addition to their obvious battlefield role of bringing death from above to their enemies, aircraft can also be used for reconnaissance. A recon aircraft flying over the tabletop might highlight the enemy's hidden reserves, or possibly even be tricked by the various 'dummy' tank and truck ruses employed, notably by the British.

One final point here is that you don't actually *need* to own any model aircraft to incorporate aerial support into your games. The speed at which they fly over the battlefield, combined with their 'whoosh and gone' presence, means that you can abstract their effect without the need to place a model. That said, there are some very nice 1:72, 1:144, and 1:300 scale aircraft on offer!

A snapshot of the many aircraft used in the Desert War is shown in the table below.

Aircraft of the Desert War

Aircraft	Nation	Role	Crew	Notes
Hawker Hurricane	Britain	Fighter / ground support	1	
Supermarine Spitfire	Britain	Fighter	2	Superior fighter.
Bristol Beaufighter	Britain	Fighter	2	
Bristol Blenheim	Britain	Bomber	3 or 4	
Messerschmitt Bf 109	Germany	Fighter	1	Superior fighter.
Messerschmitt Me 110	Germany	Fighter / ground support	2	
Junkers Ju 88	Germany	Bomber	2 to 6	Useful multi-role aircraft.
Junkers Ju 87 Stuka	Germany	Dive Bomber	2	Much feared by ground forces but vulnerable to fighters.

Aircraft	Nation	Role	Crew	Notes
Fiat CR 42	Italy	Fighter	1	Biplane.
Savoia-Merchetti SM79 Sparviero ('Sparrowhawk')	Italy	Bomber	5 or 6	
Curtiss P40	US	Ground support	1	
Douglas Havoc	US	Bomber / ground support	3	Known as Boston in British service.
Martin Baltimore	US	Bomber	4	

Special Forces and Recon Units

A number of 'special' units were deployed by both sides in North Africa. These were not always 'special forces' as we may think of them today – the 'rush in and blow 'em up' types beloved of action movies – but more often acted as the eyes and ears of their generals. That said, most of these units consisted of pretty tough hombres, well motivated and ready for action, and usually equipped with the best equipment their army could provide (or, in some cases, what they could 'acquire' without signing the correct quartermaster's chits).

Examples of such units include:

- The British Long Range Desert Group, who operated deep in the desert and behind enemy lines as recon and raiding troops.
- The British Special Air Service (SAS) who raided behind enemy lines.
- The Italian Compagnie Auto-Avio-Sahariane who raided and carried out recon behind enemy lines, with dedicated aerial support for recon and ground attack.

Alongside these, although not 'special forces' as such, the armoured cars that carried out reconnaissance missions fulfilled a similar role too. A huge variety of armoured cars were used in the Desert War – ranging from true scouting vehicles to those which were better armoured than light tanks – and they were tasked with missions ranging from true recon through to acting as defensive or protective screens ahead of, or on the flanks of, a larger force. In game terms, some rules cover reconnaissance very well – giving the player an advantage if using recon troops correctly – but if not, you may wish to consider a simple tweak along the lines of awarding initiative each turn to the player who has the higher number of armoured cars and other recon units in line of sight of enemy units. Doing so encourages you to push these units forward, giving you 'eyes on the ground' in a way that benefits your game play. If you choose to do this, you may wish to ignore morale tests caused by losses to such units, preventing a player who correctly uses a recon screen from becoming unrealistically hampered by such casualties (out of sight out of mind!).

A number of other regular army units were considered an 'elite' due to their superior training, morale, or standing within their own army. For example, British Guards units were generally well thought of, and the Australian and New Zealand troops in the Desert War had a reputation for toughness (sometimes with both friend and enemy!). The German Fallschirmjäger paratrooper units, who by this stage in the war fought as elite infantry, were generally well armed with the latest weaponry and well-motivated; and the Italian Bersaglieri (light infantry) were considered the elite of the Italian armed forces. The Free French Foreign Legion fought doggedly at the oasis of Bir Hakeim in the Battle of Gazala. On the tabletop, such units may be awarded morale bonuses or better unit commanders to reflect their brave battlefield performance.

Chapter Four

Choosing Your Rules

It's (almost) no exaggeration to say that more wargaming rule sets have been written for refighting the Second World War than Valentine tanks were built during the war (8,275 since you ask). And it's equally true that the quality of said rule sets varies more than the build quality of British and Italian tanks during the Desert War. So, which should you use for your games?

The simple, if slightly unhelpful, answer is to find the rules that best suit the gaming experience you're after, and stick with them. But with so many rules available, finding the ones that work best for you is no easy matter. In this chapter, I look at some of the more popular sets of rules for Desert War gaming, encompassing a generous spread of gaming styles and level of battle, from man-to-man skirmishing right up to divisional-level operations.

Various 'levels' of wargame may be played with the Desert War providing your backdrop, and knowing which is your preference will make a difference to the rules you try and also to the size of model you collect:

- **Squad:** The smallest level of wargame suited to the Second World War; each player takes control of a handful of models, each representing one soldier, who moves, fights, and otherwise acts independently of his chums. Such games usually involve an element of roleplaying, or reflect the small actions fought by special forces raiders against enemy camp or fortification guards. Squad-level games are usually played using 28mm or 20mm (1/76) models, and the individual weapons of each soldier should be accurately represented on each model. A radical interpretation of squad-level involves a handful of tanks fighting one-on-one.

- **Platoon:** A slight step up from squad-level games, platoon-level wargames tend to be 'big skirmish' games, with each player fielding an infantry platoon's worth of models, sometimes with additional support from heavier machine-guns, mortars, and occasionally even a solitary tank – although the latter is for the most part unrealistic in the desert. Units tend to be based around squads of ten or so models, each of which moves and acts as one; overall command is based around a Platoon HQ squad. 28mm, 20mm, and 15mm models are popular in this level of wargame.
- **Company:** Moving up, Company level games focus on the actions fought out by a company of 3–4 infantry platoons, with support once again from machine-gun platoons, mortar detachments, and a handful of tanks. Gameplay is still usually based around individual squads, although morale and general orders may be determined at platoon level. This is the smallest level of engagement where off-table artillery may play a role, but as with the inclusion of tanks in smaller level games, this is for the most part unrealistic. 20mm, 15mm, and 10mm models are most commonly used for company-level games, although 28mm games on a large table look suitably impressive.
- **Battalion:** Games at this level involve several companies of infantry, supported with artillery (on-table and off-table), heavy weapons platoons, and larger tank formations. It's possible that aerial support may play a part, too. Individual units most often represent platoons or whole companies, with the activities of individual soldiers no longer relevant to the overall outcome of the game. 15mm, 10mm, and 6mm models are frequently used for this level of game.
- **Brigade and Division:** The highest level of wargame usually played with miniatures features brigades or divisions, with the individual units representing entire companies or possibly even battalions. This level of game usually features a wide range of combined arms, and the capabilities of individual weapons and equipment may be expected to be less important than the morale and leadership of individual units. 6mm and even tiny 2mm models are best used to represent the grand, sweeping ebb and flow of large-scale operations.

Of course, it is possible to play a game without worrying about how many men each unit on the tabletop represents – or even to change this between battles. In one game, a stand of five infantrymen could represent a squad; in another game they are a platoon; and in another they may represent an entire company or battalion. The same goes for model tanks, machine-guns, and artillery, for example. So long as your choice of rules presents you with an enjoyable game, and you've had fun collecting and painting your armies, the actual level of battle represented by your game needn't be relevant.

This chapter looks at some of the most interesting, popular, and playable options available to a wargamer wishing to refight battles in the Desert War.

Battlegroup

Designer: Warwick Kinrade
Publisher: Iron Fist, 2013

Battlegroup is a reasonably straightforward set of wargame rules with a few innovative twists to pep up gameplay. The rules are designed for 20mm or 15mm models, but may of course be played with larger or smaller armies also; casualties require figure removal, so it's best to play either with individually based infantrymen, or using markers to track casualties on multiple-based figures.

The game may be played at various levels from squad up to battalion; the core rules do not change, but the amount of control and number of orders a player may give each turn rises with the level of action played (which is a good thing, as the number of units will increase too). The way orders are given creates some tabletop uncertainty every turn – you must roll a certain number of dice (from 1 in squad-level games to 4 in battalion-level games) and add to this the total number of officers you have on the table. This indicates how many actions you may take in a turn – meaning that your force's impetus will vary at different times in the game and requiring you to prioritize your actions every turn. This is a nice touch that adds plenty of tension to a battle without drowning the players in a sea of gimmickry.

Shooting is broken down into two types of fire: area fire and aimed fire. Once again, this adds a thematic decision for players – do you use area fire to pin the enemy but inflict lighter damage, or aimed fire to try to knock out specific targets (which is much harder to achieve)?

In addition to the standard type of morale rules for individual units (deciding whether they become pinned or rout if they take damage), *Battlegroup* includes a 'Battle Rating' system. Each force begins a game with a BR of between 1 and 5, and an experience level (Inexperienced, Regular, Veteran, or Elite). As casualties build or specific events take place (such as aerial attacks or senior officer being killed), a player must choose randomly selected counters numbered from 1 to 5. When the counter's overall total exceeds your BR, your force breaks. To add an element of chaos, some counters have no number, instead initiating a special event in gameplay (such as air attacks, ammo running out, or extra actions).

Alongside the core rules, players need to purchase campaign-specific supplements to provide the detailed stats and special rules for each theatre. At the time of writing, a Desert War supplement has been planned but not yet released, but the *Battlegroup Blitzkrieg* is a suitable primer for early Desert War forces.

Blitzkrieg Commander

Designer: Peter Jones
Publisher: Specialist Military Publishing, 2004

This revelatory rule set came into being after Peter Jones made the inspired decision to take an ancients/fantasy wargame (Rick Priestley's *Warmaster*), and rework it for (historical) twentieth-century battles from company right up to division level. Gone were the armour penetration charts of the rules I'd previously used, replaced with a simple but effective armour saving roll. Gone was the clunky interaction between infantry and armoured units – guns are guns in *Blitzkrieg Commander*, and the challenge is to deliver the greatest weight of firepower onto your targets of choice, with less focus on the actual weapons you're delivering it with. And the ability of commanders came to the fore, whereas most Second World War games I'd previously played placed more emphasis on the technical data and hardware of battle.

Gameplay is streamlined and simple, with your chances of destroying enemy units increasing the more firepower you can lay down on a target. Movement and morale are equally straightforward. The rules are driven by the command mechanism. Each player's force has a single Commanding Officer and several Headquarters units; every turn, the player chooses one of these, chooses which nearby units it will give orders to, and then rolls for success (depending on your army, a CO or HQ's Command Value will vary, usually between 7 and 10). If successful, the selected units take their action, and the CO or HQ may then give them another order; every successive order suffers an additional –1 to the commander's Command Value. Once an order is failed, the player moves on to his or her next CO or HQ. This is a simple but incredibly effective method of modelling the differences in command structure and initiative – for example, an Afrika Korps force is likely to get several additional actions each turn compared with a British or Italian force. So you can field Rommel's army with its Command Value of 10 and watch his panzers roll over any enemy formation put against it, even with a much smaller starting force. There's also room for tweaking the Command Values in friendly, non-points games… for a Brigadier having a bad day, lower the CO's rating by 1, and for well-planned assault by troops confident in their commander, raise it by 1.

Although incredibly well-suited to modelling combined-arms tactics, I've hosted many thrilling games of *Blitzkrieg Commander* that involve tank-only forces. The way that orders work, and the choice of spreading your firepower thinly to suppress many enemies or delivering a single sledgehammer blow to knock out just a handful, captures the feeling of movement and ebb and flow of armoured engagements in the desert. As the rules for tank combat are very simple (basically all units – AFV or otherwise – are distilled down into movement, firepower, armour, and damage-taken stats), this allows you to fight large tank battles with each model representing a single tank on the tabletop. The ultimate in Desert War AFV skirmish gaming!

Army lists are included for all major theatres and combatants, meaning that you won't need to purchase additional army lists – everything you will need is in the rulebook, both for the North African campaign and any other theatre of war in the Second World War.

More than any other set of Second World War wargame rules I've played, *Blitzkrieg Commander* rewards skilful use of combined-arms tactics, and as such, I consider it the best set of rules available for refighting the North African campaigns. They certainly rekindled my interest in Second World War wargaming when I first tried the rules out over a decade ago.

At the time of writing, Pendraken Miniatures have announced they are to publish an updated third edition of the rules, to tie in with their line of 10/12mm miniatures.

Bolt Action

Designer: Alessio Cavatore and Rick Priestley
Publisher: Warlord Games and Osprey Publishing, 2012

Bolt Action is perhaps the most popular set of Second World War rules designed for 28mm battles, although of course they may, with a little thought, be used with any size of model.

Gameplay is provisionally set at platoon level, with added support units. This means that you'll generally field a platoon (or more) of infantry squads with all sorts of exciting units bolted on … and I thought 'Bolt Action' referred to a rifle! However, the level of support units available far exceeds what any Desert War platoon commander could have reasonably wished for – so there's an element of 'bathtubbing' in these rules: by which I mean players are referring to their army as a platoon and their individual units as squads, even though the equipment available makes the game feel as though you're fighting out a higher level of engagement using these smaller formations.

The rules are nicely streamlined and revolve around the firepower of squads (as opposed to individual riflemen), and individual support MGs and mortars, tanks and anti-tank guns. Weaponry is all important, a difference in hardware making a real difference between units, but training is also very important – the more experienced a unit (the basic levels of training being Inexperienced, Regular, and Veteran), the more Pinned markers they can absorb before it fails to enact its orders and routs from the tabletop.

Bolt Action's sequence of play is well nuanced – players place a number of dice of a distinct colour into a bag or similar opaque container; the number of dice depends on the number of units you have in play. Dice are drawn from the container one at a time and the owning player chooses one of his or her units to activate. Units may only take one action per turn, and a turn continues until all dice have been removed from the container. This throws up all sorts of tough command choices – act early and let your opponent see what you're up to, or wait patiently knowing that you may be shot to pieces before delivering your masterstroke.

Tanks and artillery are seamlessly added to gameplay, working well without being overpowered. Different nationalities have their own special rules, adding a little extra flavour to the game, and the number of special units available – which are broadly based on what was available in any given theatre or operation – provides further opportunity to make your army stand out from that of your opponent.

Bolt Action sits firmly at the 'game' end of the spectrum, as opposed to 'simulation', but the popularity of these rules and simplicity of play makes them a good choice for players new to historical wargaming.

The core rulebook includes army lists only for Europe in 1944–45; the Desert War is covered in detail in the *Duel in the Sun* supplement. This includes theatre-specific army selectors, stats for all relevant AFVs and weapons, and scenarios suitable for North Africa. There's also a *Tank* supplement, enabling you to beef up your tank crews and bring a little more personality and depth to tank models in the game.

Chain of Command

Designer: Richard Clarke
Publisher: Too Fat Lardies, 2013

Chain of Command is a set of rules for platoon-sized actions with additional support units, including mortars, AFVs, and anti-tank guns. Intended for single-based models grouped into squads, a feature of most

Too Fat Lardies rules is the concept of leadership or 'big men' – making gameplay very focused on battlefield leadership and motivation. Unlike some rules, the army lists are produced in such a way that your support unit options are sensibly limited, to prevent too much overkill in a platoon-sized tabletop action.

When it was released in 2013, *Chain of Command* caused quite a stir because of the intelligently tactical 'Patrols Phase' of the game. Instead of deploying as a standard wargame, which almost all games will do unless a scenario specifies differently, both sides play a cagey mini-game which requires them to move 'blind' units on the tabletop until contact is made with the enemy. This adds a real twist to gameplay and ensures that you need to start thinking even before you see your enemy … a nice touch.

Additionally, command challenges are thrown up every turn through the game's activation system of Chain of Command Points (as the rules describe them, the leader's ability to 'read the battlefield' and act with tactical aptitude), which along with unit activation, are generated by dice rolls each turn.

Weapon ranges are long – most rifles are able to fire the length of the table for example – and combined with unit variable movement, units going 'tactical' (in better cover), and target acquisition rules, this means that games benefit from a high (some would say, realistic) amount of cover. This is something to think about in Desert War settings, which often have a fairly open tabletop (see Chapter Three for ideas on terrain).

Publisher TFL offers free PDF Army lists online, including ones for the Desert War: a visit to their Lard Island News blog will equip you with their latest available army lists. This is a favorable way of providing theatre-specific lists when compared to the supplementary army or campaign books needed for some sets of rules. TFL also produce a growing series of 'pint-sized campaigns', which look at a specific operation or battle in detail, and how to game it over a series of linked battles.

Too Fat Lardies also produce a set of company-level rules named *I Ain't Been Shot Mum* along with a supplement for Operation Compass, and another platoon-level game entitled *Troops, Weapons and Tactics*. Too Fat Lardies also publish a platoon-level, rules-universal (ie it can be used with any set of rules), character-based campaign system called *Platoon Forward*.

Crossfire

Designer: Arty Conliffe
Publisher: Quantum Printing, 1996

Designer Arty Conliffe opens the rulebook by explaining that:

> At Historicon 1995 a friend challenged me to design a historical miniatures wargame that lacked two features present in most rulesets: rulers and fixed game turns. The result is *Crossfire*.

Crossfire is a battalion-level set of rules primarily focusing on infantry combat, where individual bases represent a squad or support section, organized into companies. Support in the form of AFVs, anti-tank guns, and heavy weapons such as large-calibre mortars and HMGs are available.

The idea of a miniatures game without movement and range measurement, or fixed turns, was pretty revolutionary. In fact, it still is in many ways. Without measuring move distances, a player is free to gradually push forward his units (or boldly move long distances one at a time), shoot, take cover, and so on until an action is failed. Failure is caused by events such as a friendly unit becoming suppressed or killed by enemy fire, failing to cause casualties with your own direct fire, failing a rally action, and so on. Due to this uncertainty of when your turn will end, sometimes it pays to make many, gradual movements but at other times a calculated gamble fares better. Self-governing impetus is a very interesting concept in wargaming, and rarely is it as well rendered as in *Crossfire*.

Given the unusual activation and turn sequences, it's pleasing to find out that the rest of the rules (for shooting, morale, and so on) are fairly straightforward and most gamers will be on familiar ground.

Tabletop terrain plays a big part in *Crossfire*, so – as mentioned above for *Chain of Command* – it's worth thinking about how to represent Desert War scenery, and Chapter Three presents ideas for this. Without cover, infantry direct fire and supporting barrages will be lethal and lead to some very short games!

The rules include army lists (or more correctly, battalion lists) and ideas for scenarios. *Crossfire* is a set of rules that generates a love or hate reaction from wargamers, and I certainly recommend finding out which side of the fence you take cover behind.

Desert Rats

Designer: Jim Wallman
Publisher: online (online search: 'jim wallman desert rats pdf')

Jim Wallman has a fine track record in releasing free, online sets of rules for the periods he plays, including this one which he designed in 1995.

Desert Rats is intended for simple platoon-level games between tanks and their mechanized support units in 1/300 scale. Each player controls one platoon, but enemies only appear on the table when they have entered spotting range (you'll need an umpire to act as a go-between for the players, to ensure that units are placed at the relevant moment). A player's platoon moves in one group, so *Desert Rats* plays at its best if there are several players on each side, chaotically stumbling around the tabletop searching for their enemies (and sometimes friends).

Shooting factors vary depending on the type of gun used, the armour or protection of the target, and the angle from which you fire (side and rear armour being easier to penetrate). Infantry come into their own by being harder to spot than tanks, making infantry-handled ATGs very tricky opponents. And once casualties start to stack up, a player may have only limited control over his or her platoon, which often starts to become a little 'sticky' or even decides to move away from the enemy.

These rules are really about maintaining formations and hitting your enemies hard when you manage to find them. The tension of a game where the umpire may place an enemy of unknown type right in front of you, and knowing that a couple of rounds of heavy gunfire may make your own troops retire, makes for a very cagey game and one that plays out in a familiar way to anyone who has read the memoirs of a Desert War tanker.

At a completely different level of gaming, the same author designed *Tank Duel* (online search: 'jim wallman tank duel pdf"). A team of players take on the individual roles of the crew of a tank, with opposing teams each controlling a single vehicle in combat. Until contact is made, a screen shields the opposing tanks from each other, although you can of course hear their orders being given which adds to the guesswork and mystery of gameplay; team mates may only discuss their actions in 4–5 second bursts of action and then they must get on with their own tasks. This is a game unlike any other tabletop tank wargame I have played, bringing a very lively party game vibe into play... for example, unless the player controlling the gunner raises his or her hand and declares 'Firing now!', the opportunity to shoot is missed. It's well worth a look, if only as an eye-opening insight into the way that a 'wargame' may be played.

Flames of War

Designer: Phil Yates
Publisher: Battlefront, 2002 (Third Edition, 2012)

The first edition of *Flames of War* was published in 2002, and in the following decade and a half, this set of rules has become arguably the most popular historical miniatures game within our hobby. Certainly, *Flames of War* dominates 15mm Second World War wargaming.

Players take command of a company or equivalent, where individual stands represent half-squads or individual support weapons. However, like *Bolt Action*, *Flames of War* allows you to field a far greater number of options of support units than would be historically likely – see the earlier entry on *Bolt Action* for more about this 'bath-tubbing'.

Flames of War pushes the idea of 'game' to the fore above and beyond being a 'historical simulation'. Even so, there's plenty to like about *Flames of War* – there's nothing wrong with a wargame that excels at gameplay more so than historical simulation (for what it's worth, I feel there's a clue in the hobby being called 'wargaming', not 'war-simulating'). Different units and equipment do retain their historical effectiveness but, for example, the relative range of weapons compared with movement rates is one area where gameplay wins out over historical data. Another example is the lack of 'battlefield friction' – if their morale is good, you can move any and all of your units as you wish without fear of your turn ending suddenly or troops refusing to do what they're told. The same can also be said of many other rules, of course, though many popular modern rule sets include some form of limitation.

The basic rules are simple and well presented, although adding in support units beyond the core infantry and AFVs does significantly increase the learning curve without ever becoming too complex a game. An example of the simple but evocative rule-writing evident in *FoW* is that when rolling dice to hit an enemy unit, a player rolls against the target's experience level rather than their own shooting ability: Conscripts are easier to register hits against than Trained units, who in turn are easier to target than Veterans – it's all about how they find cover and manoeuvre on the battlefield. Added to this, each unit is rated for its morale – from Reluctant through Confident to Fearless – which, when combined with experience levels, allows for some interesting interaction. For example, a Fearless Veteran unit will be tough to shift and hard to rout, a Reluctant Green unit the exact opposite, but units such as Reluctant Veterans can be included, representing battle-weary soldiers who know how to fight but no longer want to put themselves in the firing line. Depending on the type of army you field, your experience and morale levels are decided for you by army lists (but of course, you can change these in friendly games).

For me, *Flames of War* works at its best for infantry-versus-infantry confrontations or tank-versus-tank. I especially enjoy the way the rules represent small-unit tank combat – flank and rear attacks are important, and tanks are likely to see their crews bailing out (or suffering other temporary stoppages) in addition to straightforward knock-out 'kills'. The differences in armour thickness and the relative punch of different tanks' guns is modelled simply but effectively.

The army lists available are generous in the equipment offered to players, but are based around a specific type of force. For example, you could choose to field an Italian motorcycle company, a British Jock Column, a light or medium German panzer company, or an American Ranger company. In addition to certain core units which must be fielded, a whole gamut of options opens up to you in the form of divisional support from artillery and heavy tank platoons, through air support, to anti-tank and anti-aircraft units.

Alongside this, each force may use national characteristics relevant to their armies. Much of this feels very 'gamey' but it's certainly a novel, and far from dry, approach in helping you appreciate a difference between say, British, Australian, New Zealand, and Indian troops rather than just their choice of headgear. These rules also reflect some of the differences in training between armies (for example, early British cruiser tank units may fire on the move and deploy in 'line astern', as per their training), and some are just a light, fluffy way of bestowing morale bonuses (such as Scottish units heading into battle behind their bagpipes). National characteristics are not uncommon in wargame rules – they provide much of the period-specific flavour in many sets – but *FoW* maxes out on them.

Battlefront also produce Intelligence Handbooks to support their rules. These hardback, beautifully illustrated books present an overview of a campaign, and go on to list all of the different armies you can field, plus all of the units available to each army, their organization, and the stats for fielding them on the tabletop. Even if you don't play *Flames of War*, I think these are valuable tools for a Desert War wargamer as they present easily digestible 'wargame standard' organization charts. For *FoW* Third Edition, two Intelligence Handbooks cover the Desert War:

- *Hellfire and Back! Early War Battles in North Africa (1940–1941)*
- *North Africa and the Mediterranean (1942–1943)*

However, it's easy to fall into the trap of thinking you must field 'official' forces in *Flames of War* – this perhaps happens more with these rules than any other, because the lure of the Intelligence Handbook is so strong. Great games of *FoW* may be played putting together your own forces and using the core rules for a simple and fun wargame. Just don't expect to walk into an official tournament using your own historically researched army lists (but let's not open that can of worms!).

Iron Cross

Designer: Stuart McCorquodale and Darrel Morton, with Mark Mainwaring
Publisher: Great Escape Games, 2015

The concept of *Iron Cross* sounds purpose-built for the Desert War: a set of rules allowing you to field 'loads of armour with supporting infantry'. The level of game is rather open, although provisionally one tank model represents one real tank, support weapons and ATGs represent two or three such weapons, and a base of infantry figures represents a single squad.

Play focuses on taking and commanding the battle's initiative. When holding the initiative, a player activates units (mostly individual tanks), and continues to play until he or she wishes to pass initiative to the enemy. Why would you do this? Because once initiative passes over, it's your enemy's turn to have at you… and each of your units may only act once per turn. By taking a few actions, and holding back some of your units to activate later in the turn, you'll have a chance to strike back against your opponent, rather than watching them act without being able to intervene. All very simple but also very challenging for each player!

Iron Cross is very unfussy when it comes to data crunching and rule mechanisms; tanks are divided into light, medium, and heavy, and are also rated for armour, weapon power, and morale. Various units of infantry and support weapons are available, but there's no distinction between nationalities (unlike some Second World War games).

No Desert War army lists are available at the time of writing, but a supplement is planned for release in the near future. However, using the AFV charts in Chapter Two, it is easy enough to design your own tank stats to bring *Iron Cross* into North Africa.

KISS Rommel

Designer: Norman Mackenzie
Publisher: online (online search: 'KISS Rommel wargame')

KISS Rommel (KISS = 'Keep It Simple, Stupid") offers you the chance to command the entire Afrika Korps or Eighth Army across the full expanse of the Western Desert campaign in 1941–42. And to do so for free, as designer Norman Mackenzie kindly placed his rules online for us to share.

You field either four or five full divisions, each comprising around a dozen battalions (each base of models you field equals one such battalion), and take the fight to your opponent on a 6x4 tabletop representing a large area of North Africa, edged at one side by the Mediterranean Sea and on the other by the Southern Desert. The rules are intended for 6mm (or the even tinier 2mm) models, but if you have a very large playing area, you might be able to use larger scale models to KISS Rommel with.

Your forces are chosen from randomly selected cards, representing such large scale formations as the German 15th Panzer Division, Italian Savona Infantry Division, or the British 4th (Indian) Infantry Division or 7th Armoured Division. This is battle on a grand scale!

Given the level of engagement being fought, it's no surprise that troop types are limited: HQ, Recon, Tanks (British have Infantry and Cruiser tanks), Motorized Infantry, Foot Infantry (Italian only), Artillery, and 88mm ATGs (Germans only). In effect, your army is distilled down into the most critical troop types of the campaign, and all other support units are assumed to be present without needing models to represent them (so for example, infantry divisions have their support companies, attached artillery, and so on, all factored into their values). Minefields may be laid and removed, and extra points are awarded for capturing enemy supply depots.

The battle rules are very straightforward, and optional rules add flavour (such as airstrikes and Italian command problems); a mini campaign is also included, where you must push your enemy back over a series of battles. A nice touch here is that the British player must rename his or her commander after any major defeat – because as the designer notes, 'they were constantly replaced!'

Operation Squad

Designer: Massimo Torrani and Valentino Del Castello
Publisher: Massimo Torrani, 2009

Unlike the other rules listed in this chapter, *Operation Squad* (as the name suggests) is a squad-level skirmish wargame, where each player commands around 10–12 models. It's designed to be used with 28mm models, but can easily be played with individually based 20mm or 15mm figures.

Each model acts individually and independently; the actual weapon a model is armed with makes a difference when shooting or fighting at close quarters, and a variety of characteristics may be applied to your models. One such example is the Leader characteristic, which allows friends within 20cm to use the Leader's stats; or Silent Weapon, which allows the user to remain hidden when using it (great for commando raids). Differences in weapons mostly reflect accuracy or rate of fire; in a user-friendly way, the differences between, say, a Sten and a Thompson SMG, or a Bren and an MG34 LMG, are modelled in the rules.

Play evolves from a series of actions and counter-actions: the first player nominates a model on his or her side and says what it will do; the opposing player then gets the choice of counter-acting; both players may counter one another for a maximum of three actions, and then dice to see who resolves them first. This can lead to a tense build-up of gameplay, which is excellent in a set of rules focussing on man-on-man combat.

As you might imagine for a squad-level skirmish, there are no in-depth army lists or support weapons larger than a light mortar. Suggested squads are provided for British, German, and American units (no Italians, unfortunately, but there is a Russian list) in the late war period, but these can easily be modified for use in the Desert War.

Many squad-level skirmish games are available, some very detailed and others lacking anything that makes them play differently to a Wild West shootout; few manage to achieve *Operation Squad*'s balance between simplicity of play and granular equipment detail. The fact that different weapons and skills influence the way your models fight, without resorting to an overload of in-depth tables or a sequence of play that takes five minutes to represent five seconds of real life action, means that they are well suited to small-scale commando raids, recon missions, and taking out enemy machinegun nests.

Panzer Korps

Designer: Manny J Granillo II
Publisher: Hoplite Research Games, 2008

Panzer Korps is a set of rules aimed at divisional-level wargames – the author noting that his aim in producing these rules was partly to allow gamers to adapt scenarios from board wargames (many of which are played at divisional level) onto the tabletop. A noble goal.

Units are generally battalions (with individual stands or tanks representing companies), and these are rated by morale, whether motorized or the amusingly named 'leg' units (they use their legs to get there, I suppose!), any heavy calibre weaponry and/or AFVs, and finally whether any decorated leaders are present in the unit.

In keeping with the grand scale of battle depicted, the rules present a top-level view of warfare – winning is as much about the morale and training of your units as their equipment, and this presents an interesting and slightly unusual take on Second World War wargaming (which is why *Panzer Korps* is included in this chapter).

At the heart of the system are Decision Dice. Each of your HQs is allocated a Decision Dice colour representing its leadership, communication systems, weapon performance, and overall will to fight. By rolling the formation's dice and comparing the result to a colour-coded chart, this outlines very simply what your formation will do in the coming turn, from a panic that freezes all action, through being able to activate variable numbers of units (depending on how successful your dice roll is), to moving plenty of units and rallying faltering troops at the same time. This system moves away from the traditional 'chrome'-based Second World War game, instead focussing on a higher level of command more concerned with strategic progress than the minutiae of bayonets and armour penetration charts.

One of the scenarios included in the rulebook is 'Drive on Benghazi' – a hypothetical battle between an attacking Italian–German force and a defending British–Indian force. A comprehensive list of AFVs fully statted up for the rules is included at the end of the book but, as a word of caution, the nomenclature of some British AFVs is a little wonky (but thankfully not impossible to translate).

Rapid Fire!

Designer: Colin Rumford & Richard Marsh
Publisher: Rapid Fire Publications, 2005 (second edition)

Reading the mainstream wargaming magazines of the late 1980s and early 1990s, a name that cropped up time and again as the author of Second World War articles was Colin Rumford of the Grimsby Wargames Society. From time to time, his articles included short, simple rules for the scenarios he wrote, and over time, these became a fully-fledged set of rules intended for singly-based 20mm models: *Rapid Fire!*

Catering for brigade-level games, the basic unit of manoeuvre in *Rapid Fire!* is the company, represented by 8–10 figures plus a vehicle, or 2–3 tanks. Intended for 'fast play' actions, the core rules are pretty straightforward, but where *Rapid Fire!* really comes into its own is when the plethora of additional detail comes into play – rules for things such as river crossings, fortifications, airborne landings, seaborne landings, aerial combat, and fighting in buildings (and sewers!) are all included in the main rulebook. But underpinning all of these facets of battle are simple rule mechanisms.

Unlike some rules, observation and spotting the enemy is very important; movement is also broken down into two phases, in the middle and end of your turn, allowing for suppressive fire in between, along with close combat and reserved fire from your opponent. This divided movement mechanism – units may only move in one phase or the other, not both – encourages companies to slowly move forward, covered by other companies ... a good example of straightforward mechanisms leading to realistic battlefield tactics.

Two supplements cover the key periods of the Desert War, presenting desert fighting rules, orders of battle and guidelines for refighting the major engagements using the *Rapid Fire* rules:

- *Rapid Fire Guide to the North African Campaign February to June 1941*, covers Rommel's arrival in Africa to Operation Battleaxe.
- *Rapid Fire Monty's Desert Battles: 8th Army's Desert Campaign, August 1942 to January 1943*, looks at the later part of the Western Desert campaign, including the action at El Alamein.

In addition, game stats for each nation's equipment and armour may be found on the publisher's website (online search: 'rapid fire wargame free downloads').

Chapter Five

Choosing Your Models

The major consideration when choosing which scale of models to build your armies from – alongside storage space – is the type of game you wish to play. If you're intending to refight squad or platoon-level engagements between mostly infantry units with the occasional AFV on the table for good measure, 28mm or 20mm models are viable. Playing company or even battalion-level wargames, with a handful or more AFVs and possibly light artillery on the tabletop, works better with 20mm, 15mm or even 10/12mm models; any games representing larger battles are generally best fought out using 10/12mm or 6mm armies.

Broadly speaking, I'd recommend:

- 28mm for small infantry-only skirmishes
- 20mm for small infantry skirmishes with one or two AFVs per side
- 15mm or 10/12mm for infantry battles with up to approximately ten AFVs per side
- 6mm for battle involving a lot of AFVs and/or artillery (6mm is known as 'micro-armour' for this reason)

Some wargame rules buck this trend – it's not uncommon to see 15mm *Flames of War* tank-only battles, and 6mm infantry-only battles (which tend to focus on the role of artillery and fortifications more so than bayonets and grenades).

Of course, there's nothing to stop you amassing a grand collection of 28mm Armoured Divisions, or a small but beautiful Long Range Desert Group in 6mm. But planning is everything – work out what you're aiming to collect based on the style of game you're after, and then look at the best choices in that scale.

In this chapter, I've broken the lists of available models into categories based on the average height of an infantrymen. Aside from the difference in bulk of the different ranges (and confusingly, sometimes even overall height despite the size they're marketed as!), accompanying AFVs are usually referred to by their scale ratio. As scale ratios should be more consistent in measurement than sculpted humans are, it's no surprise that several scale ratios broadly fit with certain model sizes. The common matches are shown in the table below, but really, it's best to test your choice of models out against one another to see if they 'look' right or wrong.

Infantry model size	Usable AFV scale ratios
28mm	1:60, 1:56, 1:48
20mm	1:87, 1:76, 1:72
15mm	1:110, 1:100
10 and 12mm	1:200 (10mm), 1:160, 1:144 (12mm)
6mm	1:300, 1:285

The basing of your models also has an effect: even if you have a perfect match between model height and scale ratio, if your models are based, they're going to appear 'taller' against the model AFVs than in real life. You may choose to ignore this, or find models that are scaled better for wargaming than modelling (for example, *Flames of War* AFVs often seem a little too tall in scale terms, but 'look right' when next to *Flames of War* infantrymen). Another option is to model all AFVs on a similar height of base to your infantrymen – wargamers can argue about the pros and cons of this for hours, but basically it comes down to personal preference about the 'look' you're after. I prefer based AFVs, partly for the reason mentioned above, but also for the added protection the model gains (you can pick it up by its base rather than by the hull or turret), and for ease of storage (bases can be magnetized and/or give a regular model footprint when placing into a box).

Although I focus on desert-equipped ranges in the following lists, remember that, despite most 'Desert War' ranges kitting their infantrymen out in shorts and hot weather gear, some battles (for example, some of the actions fought at night, in the winter months, and also in the different climate zones of Tunisia) saw the men wearing much heavier clothing. It's difficult to resist the lure of the 'classic' desert look, but for some battles, collecting units dressed in more temperate kit works just fine.

Inevitably, published lists of model manufacturers date quickly – companies go out of business, others arrive, and some stop selling certain ranges from time to time. What follows is not a comprehensive listing of all available models at the time of writing, but a selection of popular and/or easily available ranges to get started with or to fill gaps in your current collection (avoiding some of the harder to put together 1:72 and 1:76 'military model' kits that many wargamers have needed to rely on for decades). An online search of 'WW2 desert minis' suffixed with your chosen size of model will throw up additional manufacturers.

Unless otherwise stated in the entry, these models are metal (or metal and resin vehicles).

28mm Ranges

Artizan Design

Artizan's metal figures are some of the most characterful 28mm models around. Offering regular British, American, German, and Italian infantry ranges, these are backed up by some nice novelties: French Foreign Legion, British Commandos in the Mediterranean, the Long Range Desert Group, and a whole host of 'Pulp' characters that you may find a use for. No heavy weapons are offered.

Battle Honours

More traditionally sized at 25mm rather than 28mm, Battle Honours' models do not always mix well with other ranges, but offer a solid range of nicely posed models for the major combatants. Infantry are sold in squad packs, with a reasonable selection of command models and support weapons to back them up, plus a few extras such as motorcycle teams and infantry guns.

Blitzkrieg Miniatures

An excellent selection of AFVs, covering the most common types by all armies in the Desert War; compatible with the Perry Miniatures infantry range.

Company B

A pretty comprehensive range of AFVs scaled to match 28mm figures, Company B include all of the most common tanks, a wide range of armoured cars, plus artillery pieces and their crew.

Crusader Miniatures

Crusader have a small but nicely sculpted Second World War range, but only the American range really caters for the Desert War, being suitable for the Tunisian campaign.

Perry Miniatures

The Perry Twins are considered by many wargamers to be the best sculptors of naturally posed miniatures out there; as such, their Second World War range is well worth a look. Currently they offer French (Foreign Legion, Vichy, and Senegalese), British and Commonwealth, and Afrika Korps ranges for the Desert as metal castings, and two boxes of excellent, multi-pose hard plastic British 'Desert Rats' and Afrika Korps platoon boxes (each box containing a full platoon including command and light support weapons). A growing range of infantry guns, ATGs, and light AFVs supports the range.

Rubicon

At the time of writing, Rubicon offer British Crusader tanks; American M3 halftracks and M4 Shermans; and German Panzer IIIs, IVs, Tigers, and halftracks.

Warlord Games

Warlord Games support their *Bolt Action* rules (see Chapter Four) with a substantial range of infantry, artillery, and AFVs for all of the major combatants in the Desert War. Their range continues to grow, and is perhaps the most comprehensive in 28mm. In addition, they offer paint sets for each core army.

Westwind Productions

Westwind's Berlin or Bust range provides a small selection of nicely animated British, Indian, German, and Italian infantry and medium machine-guns for the Desert War. In addition, a number of AFVs and artillery designed for their NW European theatre range may be used for the later part of the Desert War.

20mm Ranges (including 1/72 and 1/76)

AB Figures

Although not for the North African theatre, AB produce excellent Second World War models; of most interest to a Desert War gamer are the tank crews that will add a little humanity to your iron beasts!

Airfix

Many wargamers started out in the 1970s and 1980s with Airfix Eighth Army and Afrika Korps soft plastic soldiers, and they remain popular despite the plethora of alternatives currently available. A number of other boxes – such as the Australian and Italian infantry – may be used to add variety. Many aircraft are available (model aircraft kits being the mainstay of Airfix's business), and a number of suitable tanks and artillery sets enter and leave the company's production rotation at different times – including the Tiger, Sherman, Lee/Grant, Bren carrier with 6pdr, and Panzer IV.

Armourfast

Easy-to-build hard plastic AFVs only, including two marks of Panzer III and Panzer IV, a British Crusader and Valentine, and a variety of M4 Shermans. Excellent wargamer's choice if you are looking to field these tanks!

Early War Miniatures

A great range of infantry, artillery, and AFVs for British, German, French, and Italian armies, including units such as Indian and Italian Colonial infantry. Figures may be purchased individually or in unit packs, and AFVs, ATGs, and other artillery are well catered for.

Grubby Tanks

Under the Grubby umbrella are the older Kelly's Heroes and Britannia ranges alongside Grubby's own 20mm offerings. The Kelly's Heroes and Britannia ranges provide American, Italian, British, and German infantry, while the Grubby Tanks catalogue (unsurprisingly) provide support from an extensive range of AFVs.

Esci

Soft plastic Afrika Korps, Eighth Army, and American 'Big Red One' boxes. These models were also marketed by Italeri and Revell (who produced a set of Scottish infantry too). Caesar, Waterloo 1815 and HaT produce compatible Italian infantry boxes.

Frontline

In addition to a wide range of resin scenery, Frontline sell many [resin] AFVs suitable for American, Italian, German, and British forces in the Desert War.

Lancashire Games

A range of infantry including British Eighth Army, Italians, Americans, and Afrika Korps.

Lancer Miniatures

Offering a small but growing range of AFVs to accompany a nice selection of infantry miniatures covering the British, Germans, Italians, and Americans.

Plastic Soldier Company

Although focussed on 15mm models, a growing number of PSC's hard plastic AFVs are also offered for 20mm games, including Panzer IIIs, Panzer IVs, Sherman, and the British A9 cruiser tank. At the time of writing, no Desert War infantry sets are available in 20mm.

Ready To Roll

This range of AFVs is sold by the *Rapid Fire!* rules team, offering a wide variety of tanks and other vehicles for the Desert War campaign.

S Model

A limited but lovely, easy-to-put-together range of hard plastic AFVs suitable for the Desert War, including unusual options such as the British A13 cruiser, Italian L3/33 light tank (and flamethrower variant), and German Panzer II.

SHQ

SHQ offer a very good range of infantry units and support weapons, and artillery and AFVs, for the main armies of the Desert War. Their infantry have a great variety of poses and stances.

Wargames Foundry

Perhaps the finest of all the 20mm figures listed in this chapter, Wargames Foundry's 'World War 2' range is frustratingly small (and will not be expanded). Sculpted by the renowned Perry Twins, a number of suitable packs of single or limited-pose models are available: Afrika Korps; Italian infantry and Askaris; French Foreign Legion; Australian, Indian, and British infantry; SAS; and US infantry. This range is infantry only, and includes a limited number of support weapons.

WarTime Miniatures

WarTime offer infantry ranges for the Germans, British, Italians, and (being an Australian company) Australia. In addition to infantry squads and support weapons, a number of artillery pieces are offered as well.

15mm Ranges

Battlefront

Producing a range of both metal and plastic models to support their *Flames of War* rules, Battlefront offer a very extensive and complete catalogue for the British, Americans, Germans, and Italians, including a great selection of Commonwealth troops for British players. Tanks, transport, air support, artillery, and infantry are all well catered for, and these models are sold as complete units for the company's rules (such as an infantry platoon or company; individual guns or a complete battery).

Command Decision

This range covers the major armies of the Desert War, offering infantry, artillery, and AFVs. Infantry are sold in large packs – fifty figures – so are generally best suited to players who collect big armies. The tanks and other vehicles are well cast, but are sold in packs of three, so again cater for bigger games.

Eureka Miniatures

This Australian company manufactures small but very well sculpted ranges of Australian and Italian infantry for the Desert War.

Forged in Battle

A growing range of well sculpted infantry, artillery, and AFVs. The tanks are moulded with integral bases, which some gamers will love and others will hate, but the models themselves are excellent. The range currently covers some of the more common AFVs from the Desert War (Lee/Grant, Sherman, Stuart, Panzer III, Panzer IV), rarer iconic tanks such as the Tiger and Churchill, plus halftracks and some armoured cars. Artillery is well catered for, but at the time of writing, we await infantry in desert kit.

Peter Pig

Marketing their figures as having 'more oink' than any other manufacturer – a statement we should not question – Peter Pig have an excellent range of infantry for the major armies of the Desert War. A limited selection of artillery and AFVs are also offered, but their infantry and platoon and company support weapons are fairly comprehensive. Peter Pig's packets of figures are sold in eights (or similar quantities), thus making them easier than say, Battlefront or Command Decision, for collecting smaller forces.

Plastic Soldier Company

PSC produce a superb 15mm (and 20mm) hard plastic range, including Panzer IIIs, Panzer IVs, Tigers, Churchills, Shermans, and A9 and A10 cruiser tanks plus a small range of artillery (including a 25pdr and quad tractor). At the time of writing, no Desert War infantry sets are available in 15mm.

Zvezda

A number of easy-to-build, cost effective, soft plastic tanks are offered by Zvezda: these are very much wargamer's models with enough detail to look good on the tabletop without being over fiddly. The range includes suitable British, German, and American AFVs. Although also producing infantry in soft plastic, these are 20mm, and sadly not suitable for the Desert War.

10mm and 12mm Ranges

Arrowhead Miniatures

Originally sold as the 'Wargames South' range, Arrowhead's AFVs have excellent detail, and are supported by artillery and infantry sets. The German, American, and British AFV ranges present most of the vehicles required for the Desert War, but the Italian range is sadly lacking (only two AFVs are included). Infantry and artillery are excellent for the British and Americans but, at the time of writing, no Afrika Korps infantry are offered, and neither are Italian infantry or artillery.

Pendraken

A comprehensive range of AFVs, guns, and infantry for the British, Italians, Germans and Americans. Unlike some other 10/12mm ranges, Pendraken's AFVs mostly come as two-piece castings (chassis and hull), sidestepping the necessity to assemble these small models in kit form. This does, however, mean that some of the models are less detailed than kit-form AFVs. Of the available 10/12mm ranges, Pendraken's extensive range is perhaps the best place to start with regard to choices for raising a combined-arms force.

Pithead

Pithead produce an excellent range of tanks and other AFVs for all the major combatants, along with suitable infantry and support weapon packs.

Miniature Figurines

Minifigs have a good selection of models for the major armies, featuring AFVs, artillery, and infantry. These are more delicately sculpted models than most other 10/12mm ranges, so do not always mix well (this is especially true of the infantry) – although the models on offer will provide most of your needs without the necessity to mix and match manufacturers.

Skytrex

Skytrex's 'Action 200' range is, as the name suggests, scaled at 1/200 (so is not compatible with the other ranges included here). However, it offers a pretty comprehensive range of tanks, infantry, and artillery for the major armies of the Desert War, and the tanks are especially appealing.

6mm Ranges

C-in-C

Offering a good range of German and US AFVs, transport, artillery and infantry, C-in-C's range for the British and Italians is less complete. These are well-sculpted models with a good level of detail for their size.

GHQ

GHQ's vehicles are simply the best of the micro-armour ranges, true miniature works of art in 1/286 scale. Unsurprisingly, this quality comes at a cost, as GHQ are the most expensive of the 6mm ranges. The infantry are – in my opinion – a little spindly, which results in the occasional casualty in storage or on the table; some trucks and guns are rather tricky to put together as everything is scale-appropriate and sometimes rather small or fiddly; but aside from these minor quibbles, GHQ offer a superb collection of models. Comprehensive ranges are produced for the main combatants in the Desert War, including AFVs, artillery, infantry, and some aircraft.

Heroics & Ros

Heroics & Ros produce a wide range of micro-armour, infantry, and aircraft for the whole of the Second World War. Despite many of the models having been sculpted in the 1970s or 1980s, they stand up remarkably well, and are perhaps the best happy medium between GHQ and the other 6mm ranges. Their infantry are provided in rifle squad or support weapon packs, and the range of AFVs and soft-skin vehicles is excellent. British, Italian, German, and American forces are all represented in their catalogue.

Irregular Miniatures

Although not the best-detailed of 6mm ranges, Irregular's castings are rugged and well suited to gameplay (you'll break fewer gun barrels on Irregular AFVs than some other 6mm AFVs, for example, because everything is that bit chunkier). Ranges are produced for the main combatants, including AFVs, artillery, infantry, and some aircraft. A few gaps exist – no Italian M11/39 tanks, for example, but most gamers will find what they need.

Scotia

Scotia are closest in style of Heroics & Ros, although offering a very limited range of vehicles only.

Chapter Six

Scenarios

The pick-up game so beloved of wargamers – two well-balanced forces stumbling upon one another from opposite sides of a table, with no discernable objectives other than the destruction of the enemy – has its place in the hobby. Such games can be great fun, and in all honesty, are not so out of place or context in the Desert War when compared to many other periods and settings.

However, adding a few twists to the basic 'kill them all' formula adds some theatre-specific detail and frequently means that the player with the better plan for achieving his or her objectives is more likely to win than the army that fields the most 88mm ATGs (that'll be the Germans, by the way).

This chapter provides four scenarios broadly based on typical actions of the campaign, all broadly focussing on the theme of movement and manoeuvre which I feel is very evocative of the Desert War. As they're designed with no one rules set in mind and can be played at any level of battle (from skirmishes upwards), you may need to slightly adjust the length of game or some other factors. But with a little forethought or experience of your chosen rules set, a challenging game may be put together using the ideas included in this chapter.

Keep On Running

This scenario is designed for tank- or armoured car-heavy forces, and reflects the fluid, roaming style of tank combat fought throughout 1941 and much of 1942. For many wargamers, this typifies their view of the

Desert War: Crusaders, Honeys, Mark IIIs, and Mark IVs, zipping across each other's line of sight, in and out of the action's wrecked tanks.

Two forces meet while on the move – this may be one small part of a larger action, one armoured column being despatched to intercept another, or even two lighter patrols bumping into each other unexpectedly in the desert. The aim is for your force to move units off the opposite table edge to outflank or outrun the enemy, while also inflicting the heaviest casualties you can.

Both forces should be fairly equal in point values; neither side plays the 'defender' in this scenario – it is out-and-out attack! Ideally each side will have six to eight units on the table; depending on the scale of battle you wish to fight, a 'unit' could comprise a single AFV, a troop of three to five tanks, or a larger formation such as a squadron. Scaling up further, you could even choose to refight the flank of one of the major battles of the campaign, with each unit representing a much larger force.

Setting up the table

This scenario is very simple to set up; play it across a fairly open table, without the need for any major terrain features. Both players may place a handful of terrain pieces, but generally keep lines of sight long and provide little cover to hide behind. This will be a short, sharp action!

I recommend playing diagonally across your table, which has the effect of elongating flanks and adding depth to your deployment. After the minimal terrain has been set up, the side with the greater number of light tanks and armoured cars chooses one corner to deploy in; their opponent must choose that opposite.

Victory conditions

Play for a set number of turns; this will vary depending on your rule set of choice, but six to eight turns is usually enough to reach a decisive outcome.

At the end of the game, each player scores points as follows:

- 1 point for each enemy unit destroyed or routed.
- 3 points for every two of your units exiting the table before the start of the final turn.
- 1 point for every two of your units exiting the table during the final turn.

Units exiting the table for victory purposes must move off the table (not rout) through the enemy's initial deployment zone.

The player with the higher total wins.

Rules considerations

This scenario is a great way to use the many and varied tanks and armoured cars you will undoubtedly collect. Some units may need to be larger than others to account for differences in the points values of opposing AFVs.

You may choose to rule that only units at half strength or above may be counted when moving off the table for victory purposes. This discourages ploughing through the enemy in a straight line regardless of casualties… a badly shot up unit arriving at its final destination on the battlefield will be of little use.

With only six to eight units per side, you'll need to think hard over the best time to move units off the table for maximum benefit, without reducing your on-table firepower too dramatically.

Into the Valley of Death

This scenario is broadly based on the various actions fought at Halfaya Pass during Operations Brevity (May 1941), Skorpion (May 1941), and Battleaxe (June 1941); and the near destruction of 17/21st Lancers (in Valentine IIIs and Crusader IIIs) at Thala during the Battle of Kasserine Pass in February 1943.

The attacking force is mechanized, and needs to move down the length of the table to capture several objectives from the defending enemy (which may be mechanized or not, defender's choice).

The attacking force may be either Allied or Axis, although it does seem that the Allies were more likely to make this kind of assault. The attacking force should outnumber the defending force (in either points or number of units) by approximately 2:1. This style of battle lends itself well to company or higher-level games, but there's no reason that it won't work as a (pretty bloody) skirmish, also.

Setting up the table

Play down the length of your table – the shorter sides are each force's baseline. I recommend that the defender sets up fairly limited terrain, consisting of hills that must be in contact with a table edge, plus a handful of areas of broken ground (that both impede movement and give limited cover). Once this is done, the attacker then gets to place a few patches of scrub (counting as cover), and perhaps a wadi (again, providing cover). The overall table feel should be fairly open, enclosed by hills around the sides, with some limited cover for the attacker down the middle of the table.

Three objective markers are then placed on the table – whoever holds more at the end of the game will be the winner. One objective must be within 1 tank move of the defender's baseline (placed by the defender); the other two must be placed between two and three tank moves from the defender's baseline (placed by the attacker). Of course, depending on your table size and distances moved within your rules of choice, this may need some tweaking.

Your objectives may be anything that stands out – command posts, fuel dumps, and so on; they should cover an area no larger than a beermat or drink coaster. There are some excellent resin objectives available in 15mm, designed for Flames of War.

Once the objectives are deployed, the defender can deploy his or her units across the area between the defender's baseline and the forward-most objective. If playing using a points system, the defender may purchase light defences such as trenches, gun pits, etc, but not heavy fortifications such as pill boxes. Minefields may be deployed.

The attacker then deploys within 1 move of the attacker's baseline and takes the first move of the game.

Victory conditions

This scenario works best if played for a set number of turns, otherwise the attacking force is likely to sit back and engage in a gunnery duel to break the enemy's morale rather than moving forward to get boots on the objectives. I recommend playing for a number of turns equal to approximately one and a half times the minimum number of moves an average speed attacking unit would take to cross the board (for example, a unit that moves 6" per turn would be allowed 18 turns to cross a 6ft table). This means that the attacker must keep moving some units forward while keeping up as much suppressing fire as possible.

To hold an objective, a unit must be the sole occupant at the end of a turn. If both players have elements of a unit (no matter how weak or strong) contesting the objective's footprint, neither side holds it.

Whichever player holds more objectives at the end of the game wins; if neither player has a foothold on a particular objective, it is not counted. If both players hold 1 objective at the end of the game, it is a stalemate.

Should one player's force rout before the end of the game due to a morale test – or be completely wiped out – the opposing player is considered to hold all three objectives and therefore wins the game.

Rules considerations

If the attacking force is a British one primarily equipped with 2pdr tank guns, unless the defending force also primarily consists of tanks, this is going to be pretty one-sided! As noted elsewhere in this book, the 2pdr was not equipped with HE rounds, so British tanks equipped thus relied on machineguns for anti-personnel and anti-ATG attacks… meaning they will be desperately outgunned by Axis artillery. If the defending force is mostly infantry and ATGs, give the British overwhelming numbers – the 'joy' of this game will be discovering whether the British can move close enough to use their machineguns before being wiped out. For any other army, this is less of an issue.

Given the importance of cover in this scenario, discuss with your opponent the exact type of cover and sight-blocking offered by each piece of terrain on the board. Ensure that both players are clear about this before deployment.

To encourage combined-arms tactics, you may agree before the game that objectives may only be 'held' by infantry units. This adds an extra tactical dimension to the scenario, requiring both players to manoeuvre infantry (whether motorized or on foot), keeping them intact while pushing them into position.

Other than this, the key to a good game with this scenario is to balance the forces correctly. Most rules with points values help you to achieve this, and although I've recommended that the attacking force should outnumber the defending force by approximately 2:1, you may wish to experiment with differing ratios to allow one side or the other a better chance of success.

Hit the Convoy

The Desert War was as much about supply lines as it was about direct action. Every battlefield success and advance stretched the victor's distance from their rear bases, and at times, the momentum of attack could be lost if reserve men and materiel could not be delivered to the front in good time. Therefore, what went on behind the front line had a huge impact on the course of the campaign, and the vast expanses of North Africa allowed units from either side to operate deep behind enemy lines before detection. Closer to the front line, flanking moves and sudden breakthroughs could endanger the enemy's supply routes. Fast moving AFVs or aircraft could catch a supply column unawares with devastating effect; guarding a convoy was never glamorous work, but could certainly be dangerous!

This scenario is best played at platoon or company level, although squad-level games could depict an attack on a handful of enemy trucks or, at battalion level or higher, this scenario could be used to represent the type of action fought at Beda Fomm.

Both sides can be of equal strength, or the attacking force can be slightly larger – if this is the case, make it easier for the convoy to escape by starting it further along its route or offering more than one exit point. The convoy vehicles (outlined in Victory Conditions) should not count towards the defender's points value.

The attacking force may be either Allies or Axis, and will most likely have a higher proportion of tanks and armoured cars than the convoy's escort, which most likely contains plenty of truck or halftrack-mounted infantry, some towed artillery, and light tanks or armoured cars.

Setting up the table

Play takes place lengthways down the longest distance your tabletop allows. Ideally a road or desert track will run from one end to the other in a fairly straight line, and the majority of the table will be open, good going. Patches of rough ground and other cover are fine, and a few hills scattered along the table's flanks provide a perfect site for the attacking force to advance into view over.

The defender first deploys his or her convoy vehicles in a line along the road, starting with the rearmost model in contact with the base edge. The number of vehicles used will depend on the size of your table and the number of models you have available. Around the convoy, the defender then deploys the protecting units, no more than one move's distance from the convoy. One or two units may be held off the table to follow on behind the last vehicle.

With no attacking forces deployed, the defender then takes the first move of the game. Once this is taken, the attacker then deploys around 75 per cent of his or her force along one of the table's long sides, and the remainder on the opposite table edge – this represents the main ambushing force and a backstop or decoy shadowing the other flank. Deployment counts as the attacker's phase in the first turn, so play then returns to the defender, who may move but may not shoot in the second turn (the shock of enemy raiders appearing means that they're busy loading, calling for help, and so on)! After that, play continues as normal within your rules.

Victory conditions

The defender aims to get convoy vehicles to safety off the table edge opposite his or her starting edge. Every vehicle leaving the table gains the defender 5 points (unless the model routs off the table, which counts for nothing).

The attacker gets 2 points for every convoy vehicle destroyed or captured.

This skewed victory point system usually balances out fairly well in practice, as it is easier for the attacking force to knock out convoy vehicles at longer distances.

Rules considerations

The road or track won't provide any movement bonus except to allow unhindered travel through rough terrain. Even so, you may wish to rule that the convoy vehicles cannot leave the road until they have been fired upon or have taken casualties.

To prevent convoy vehicles unrealistically sailing past enemy units in close proximity, you may rule that convoy models must stop if going within one move's distance of enemy units – this forces them to take a wide berth.

The defenders may give the attacking force a nasty surprise by mixing troop trucks (sometimes with AA or AT guns mounted) in with the convoy vehicles. The defending player will need to note which is which, and may reveal each model's cargo at any time – preferably at short range against an unsuspecting enemy.

To make things even trickier for the attacker, you may wish to simulate a night attack, reducing the distance over which units may shoot. Or if things go too easily for the defender, next time you play, allow the attacker some aerial support to shoot up the convoy with at the start of the first turn.

Deep into Enemy Territory

This scenario can be fought at several levels of gameplay: as a man-on-man skirmish, it could represent an incident along the lines of 1941's Operation Flipper, where a small party of British commandos assaulted a building thought to be Rommel's headquarters (he wasn't there and it didn't go too well for the commandos); as a small unit battle, it could be the British LRDG, the Italian Compagnie Auto-Avio-Sahariane, or similar, driving into an airfield or supply dump to cause chaos; or on a larger scale, the raid might be a diversionary attack as part of a larger operation, designed to be a noisy flash-bang distracting from activity elsewhere.

Whatever scale you play at, the key to this scenario is a defined target or targets (see the next section). The attacking force aims to capture/destroy them, and the defender must protect them at all costs. By the nature of such actions, the raiding force should be smaller than the defending force, but consists of elite units or units with high morale; the defending force is most likely of an average or slightly inferior quality. Using a points-based rule set helps you to play a balanced scenario.

You'll need a number of markers of some kind to place on the table for this scenario (up to 10 depending on the situation). Depending on the target of the raid, this could be an individual model, purpose-made objective markers, or even paper or plastic markers – whatever's easiest for you to keep track of. These are the Targets – the raiders' objective.

Setting up the table

Laying out the table will vary very much according to the type of raid you're going to play. It could be an airfield, a cluster of houses, a defended supply dump – whatever suits your theme. And the board can be as cluttered or devoid of features as you wish, again in-keeping with the raid you're carrying out.

Before deploying any models, the players next place the all-important Targets on the table. There are 10 Target Points up for grabs in the game, divided between 1–10 Target markers: as the raiding force has carefully chosen its Targets, or been given a specific mission, the attacker (raider) gets to choose how the Target Points are divided between Target markers, but the defender places them. In an assassination-style scenario, all 10 Target Points are represented by one key Target model on the table – Rommel, Montgomery, or even Hitler or Churchill if you wish to end the war in one night – whereas a raid on an airfield could see perhaps 5 or 10 Targets each worth 2 or 1 point.

The defender lays down all of the targets no more than two moves distant from the table's edge – these can be spread out or clustered as the defender wishes. The defender then places all of his or her units on the table wherever they wish.

The raider – whose units have silently lain in wait, looking for an opportunity to strike – may then attempt to move some of the defending units, representing the raider's ability to strike at an advantageous moment. The raider chooses one quarter of the table (dividing the table into quarters from the centre point) as their starting area, and rolls a six-sided die for every enemy unit deployed there. On a roll of 4+, the defender must move this unit into a different quarter, placing it no closer than 1 move from the original quarter's line.

The raider now deploys all of his or her units anywhere along the table edges of the quarter they have chosen as their starting area, and takes the first move.

Play for a set number of turns – work this out in advance by allowing a number of turns equal to that needed for the raiders to advance to the centre of the table and back again, plus an extra four turns (again, this may change according to your rules of choice). This allows for firefights, setting charges, and so on.

Victory conditions

In total, there are 10 Target Points on offer – the defender aims to keep as many of these intact as possible, while the raider aims to kill/blow up the Targets. Each Target Point won or lost by a player counts towards victory.

At the end of the final turn of the game, count up the Target Points totals gained by each side: the highest scorer wins, with any tied result counting as a draw.

Rules considerations

Three aspects of gameplay are important to this scenario, but you may not find them covered by your wargame rules of choice:

- Destroying the Targets. Some rules do cover this, but if not, agree with your opponent before the game begins exactly what is required. For an assassination it may be as simple as shooting the Target just as you would any other model – or perhaps the Target is given two or three 'wounds' to keep him or her alive for longer; perhaps even moving into contact with the Target will be required, to check he or she is definitely dead. For ammunition dumps, aircraft, and similar large Targets, most likely the raiders will need to move into contact, spend a turn setting explosive charges (without moving or firing), and the Target is destroyed in the turn that the raiding unit moves away. Some Targets may even be shot up from a distance – if this is the case, I again recommend allocating each Target a certain number of 'wounds' to destroy it.
- Sleepy or unaware defenders. Often raids would take place under cover of night, or even simply catch their target by surprise due to the distance they are 'safely' behind the front line. To reflect this, add an element of surprise – the defenders are not standing-to with fixed bayonets and loaded artillery, they're having a nap or eating their dinner. The initial advantage should lay with the raiders, so add a rule that does not allow the defender to move or shoot during the first turn of the game, or that they must roll a 4+ on a six-sided die at the start of a turn before being able to do anything (having succeeded, they no longer need to test).
- Night action. As noted above, raids of this kind often took place at night. If your rules do not already include guidelines for such battles, introduce limited lines of sight, firing ranges, and possibly even reduced movement. Depending on the style of game you're after, you could move all raiding units using hidden movement until within long or perhaps even short firing range, or introduce a few dummy units that must be identified and removed by the defender before identifying the real threats. Flares, searchlights and the light from burning fuel dumps could be added to give the defenders an increased chance of working out what has hit them!

Appendix

Further Reading

Few conflicts have had as many words written about them as the Second World War. Although seemingly less popular than the endless retelling of D-Day and beyond, or the Fall of France, there's an incredible amount of media relevant to the Desert War. The following list of books is recommended for wargaming insights and source material, with the occasional well-written or finely detailed historical overview containing useful insights for the tabletop.

Anderson, T, *The History of the Panzerwaffe, Volume 1* (Osprey, 2015).

Atkinson, R, *An Army at Dawn* (Abacus, 2004).

Battistelli, PP, *Afrika Korps* (Osprey, 2006).

Battistelli, PP, *Afrikakorps Soldier 1941–43* (Osprey, 2010).

Battistelli, PP, *Italian Army Elite Units & Special Forces 1940–43* (Osprey, 2011).

Bradford, GR, *Armour Camouflage & Markings: North Africa 1940–1943* (Arms & Armour, 1974).

Brown, J, *Colours of War* (Battlefront, 2015).

Bull, S, *World War II Infantry Tactics: Squad and Platoon* (Osprey, 2004).

Cappellano, F, and PP Battistelli, *Italian Light Tanks: 1919–45* (Osprey, 2012a).

Cappellano, F, and PP Battistelli, *Italian Medium Tanks: 1939–45* (Osprey, 2012b).

Carver, M, *Dilemmas of the Desert War* (Spellmount, 2002).

Chadwick, F, *Command Decision: Benghazi Handicap* (Test of Battle Games, 2007).

Chamberlain, P, and E Doyle, *Encyclopaedia of German Tanks of World War Two* (W&N, 1999).

Chamberlain, P, and C. Ellis, *British and American Tanks of World War Two* (W&N, 2000).

Crociani, P, *Italian Soldier in North Africa 1941–43* (Osprey, 2013).

Dando, N, *From Tobruk to Tunis: The Impact of Terrain on British Operations and Doctrine in North Africa, 1940–1943* (Helion & Co, 2016).

Delaforce, P, *Taming the Panzers* (Sutton, 2000).

Delaforce, P, *Battles with Panzers* (Sutton, 2003).

Featherstone, D, *Tank Battles in Miniature: A Wargamer's Guide to the Western Desert Campaign 1940–1942* (Patrick Stephens, 1973).

Ford, K, *El Alamein 1942* (Osprey, 2005).

Ford, K, *Gazala 1942* (Osprey, 2008).

Ford, K, *Operation Crusader 1941* (Osprey, 2010).

Ford, K, *The Mareth Line 1943* (Osprey, 2012).

Forty, G, *The Armies of Rommel* (Arms & Armour, 1997).

Griffith, P, *World War II Desert Tactics* (Osprey, 2008).

Jentz, TL, *Tank Combat in North Africa: The Opening Rounds* (Schiffer, 1998).

Holland, J, *Together We Stand: North Africa 1942–1943* (Harper Collins, 2006).

Latimer, J, *Operation Compass* (Osprey, 2000).

Lucas, J, *War in the Desert* (Arms & Armour, 1982).

Lyall, G, and B Lyall, *Operation Warboard* (John Curry edition, 2013).

Mitcham, SW, *Rommel's Desert War* (Stackpole, 2007).

Mitcham, SW, *Triumphant Fox* (Stackpole, 2009).

Molinari, A, *Desert Raiders, Axis and Allied Special Forces 1940–43* (Osprey, 2007).

Moorehead, A, *The Desert War: The Classic Trilogy on the North African Campaign 1940–43* (Aurum, 2009).

Moreman, T, *Desert Rats* (Osprey, 2007).

Moreman, T, *Desert Rat 1940–43* (Osprey, 2011).

Morisi, P, *The Italian Folgore Parachute Division* (Helion, 2016).

Munson, K, *Bombers 1939 – 1945* (Bounty Books, 2012a).

Munson, K, *Fighters 1939 – 1945* (Bounty Books, 2012b).

Perrett, B, *British Tanks in North Africa 1940–42* (Osprey, 1981).

Perrett, B, *Desert Warfare* (Pen & Sword, 2015).

Plant, J, *Cruiser Tank Warfare* (New Generation, 2014).

Plant, J, *Infantry Tank Warfare* (New Generation, 2014).

Quarrie, B, *Armoured Wargaming* (Patrick Stephens, 1988).

Restayn, J, *WWII Tank Encyclopedia in Color 1939–45* (Histoire & Collections, 2007).

Rotman, G, *M3 Medium Tank vs Panzer III: Kasserine Pass 1943* (Osprey, 2008).

Sandars, J, *British 7th Armoured Division 1940–45* (Osprey, 1977).

Sheppard, R, *The Tank Commander Pocket Manual 1939–1945* (Pool of London, 2016).

Stewart, A, *The Early Battles of the Eighth Army: Crusader to the Alamein Line* (Pen & Sword, 2002).

Suermondt, J, *Infantry Weapons of World War II* (David & Charles, 2004).

Thompson, J, *Forgotten Voices: Desert Victory* (Ebury, 2011).

Tucker-Jones, A, *Images of War: Armoured Warfare in the North African Campaign* (Pen & Sword, 2011).

Watson, BA, *Exit Rommel* (Stackpole, 2007).

White, BT, *Tanks and Other AFVs of the Blitzkrieg Era* (Blandford, 1972).

Williamson, G, *Afrikakorps 1941–43* (Osprey, 1991).

Zaloga, SJ, *US Armored Units in the North African and Italian Campaigns 1942–45* (Osprey, 2006).

Zaloga, SJ, *Kasserine Pass 1943* (Osprey, 2005).

Index